W9-DHK-892

Esmeralda Santiago and Joie Davidow

LAS CHRISTMAS

Esmeralda Santiago is the author of two memoirs, When I Was Puerto Rican *and* Almost a Woman *(both available in English and in Spanish from Vintage), and a novel,* América's Dream. *She lives in Westchester County, New York.*

Joie Davidow was a founder of the L.A. Weekly, L.A. Style *magazine, and* Sí, *a national Latino lifestyle publication. She lives in Los Angeles.*

ALSO BY ESMERALDA SANTIAGO

When I Was Puerto Rican
América's Dream
Almost a Woman

LAS CHRISTMAS

Las Christmas

FAVORITE LATINO AUTHORS
SHARE THEIR HOLIDAY MEMORIES

Edited by Esmeralda Santiago
and Joie Davidow

Illustrated by José Ortega

VINTAGE BOOKS
A Division of Random House, Inc.
New York

First Vintage Books Edition,
October 1999

Copyright © 1998 by Cantomedia, Inc., and Joie Davidow
Illustrations copyright © 1998 by José Ortega

All rights reserved under International and Pan-American Copyright Conventions. Published in the United States by Vintage Books, a division of Random House, Inc., New York, and simultaneously in Canada by Random House of Canada Limited, Toronto. Originally published in hardcover in the United States by Alfred A. Knopf, Inc., New York, in 1998.

The following essays appeared in the December 1996 issue of *Sí* magazine: "The Three Kings Lose Their Way," "PeMex Xmas," "Merry Crisis and a Hyper New Year!," "Next Year in Havana," "Nurturing the Wild Beast of Christmas," "A Baby Doll Like My Cousin Jenny's," "Barrio Humbug," and "Oy! What a Holiday!" "Switching to Santicló" first appeared in *Latina* (December 1997); "Un Poquito de Tu Amor" in the *Los Angeles Times* (February 1998).

Owing to limitations of space, all acknowledgments for permission to reprint previously published material may be found on page 199.

Vintage and colophon are registered trademarks of Random House, Inc.

The Library of Congress has cataloged the Knopf edition as follows:

Christmas (Alfred A. Knopf, Inc.)
Las Christmas : favorite Latino authors share their holiday memories / edited by
Joie Davidow and Esmeralda Santiago. — 1st American ed.
p.   cm.
ISBN: 0-375-40151-2
1. Christmas—Latin America.   2. Christmas cookery—Latin America.
3. Christmas—United States.   I. Davidow, Joie.   II. Santiago, Esmeralda.
GT4987.155.C57 1998
394.2663'089'68—dc21   98-15884
CIP

Vintage ISBN: 0-375-70155-9

Photograph by Rudi Weislein
Book design by Cassandra Pappas

www.vintagebooks.com

Printed in the United States of America
10 9 8 7 6 5 4 3 2 1

Contents

Poems and Songs

Menu

You are invited to spend Christmas at our house . . .

Introduction

IN THE SPANISH-SPEAKING AMERICAS, Christmas is much more than a one-day event followed by a staggering credit card bill. The festivities last for weeks, beginning well before Christmas, and continuing straight through to the arrival of the Three Kings and the Feast of the Epiphany on January 6. Las Navidades involves a lot more partying and a lot less shopping than a U.S. Christmas.

In Mexico, the celebration officially starts on December 16, when the wanderings of Mary and Joseph are commemorated with the *posadas*, candlelit processions which take place for the nine nights leading up to Christmas Eve. Children lead the parade, carrying a litter displaying clay figurines that represent Joseph and Mary on their burro, and the angel who followed them on their journey from Nazareth to Bethlehem. Outside the house of the evening's host, they sing the song of Joseph, asking for a place to spend the night, while inside the house, the host, playing the role of the innkeeper, sings back, turning them down, telling them to go away. At last, realizing the identity of his holy guests, the host sings a welcoming final verse, and opens the door. The party moves inside, where there are drinks, sweets—and a piñata for the children to break.

Something similar takes place in Puerto Rico, where the religious origins of the *parrandas* have been all but forgotten, while the tradition of going from house to house remains. The songs that accompany the *parrandas* refer less to the journey of Mary and Joseph and focus more on the quickly disappearing traditions of Puerto Rican rural life, including the foods typically prepared for Navidades.

In the tropical climates of the Caribbean and the temperate climes of South America, where Christmas falls smack in the middle of summer, there is no Santa arriving on a sleigh, no jingle bells in the snow, no stockings hung on the mantel with care. It's a holiday for family, for grown-ups as well as children, celebrated with plenty of traditional food, drink, music, and dance.

Nochebuena, Christmas Eve, is the night for *la misa del gallo*, "the rooster's mass," which begins at midnight. In Mexico, the mass is usually followed by fireworks and the ringing of bells, after which everyone goes home to enjoy a big feast.

Children nowadays receive gifts on Christmas Day, but they also wait until the night of January 5 to put out not their stockings but their shoes, filled with sweet grass to feed the camels. Their gifts come courtesy not of a fat man in a red suit but of *los tres reyes*, the Three Kings. The gifts of the Magi are visited upon these children, in commemoration of the gifts brought to the Christ child. The holidays finally end the next day with the Feast of the Epiphany. In Mexico, families serve the *rosca de reyes*, a traditional wreath-shape cake filled with spices, dried fruit, and one tiny doll, representing the baby Jesus. Whoever finds the doll in his or her slice has to host the next feast, which is not very far off—Candelmas, on February 2.

Traditions like these became a part of my life in my role as editor of *Sí* magazine, which folded at the end of 1996. We had a great time with that final issue, not only because we knew it would be our last, but because it focused on Christmas, and the many ways in which the holiday is celebrated in Latin America. Eight leading Latino authors were invited to contribute short Christmas memories for a special section. We attempted to offer equal time to memories from South and Central America and the Spanish Caribbean, and to memories of growing up in the States—a Mexican-American in San Francisco, a Cuban-American in Miami—where traditions are maintained, transformed, or lost. We expected to get a lovely kaleidoscope of holiday pictures, describing traditional celebrations from the many cultures labeled "Latino"—warm, fuzzy stories of singing Puerto Rican *aguinaldos*, parading in candlelight *posadas*, and feasting on Cuban *lechón*, sweet, crispy Mexican *buñuelos*, and hot chocolate *atole*.

But the stories that came back to us were not always jolly portraits of childhood celebrations. Christmas, we discovered, touches off a full range of feelings. That most highly anticipated of holidays, when families are expected to convene in an atmosphere of great abundance, perfect love, and unmitigated joy, can also be a setup for disappointment, a ripe atmosphere for drama. All the elements that make up a child's world become magnified by the exigencies of Christmas.

For a poor child there is no ecstatic Christmas morning, no tearing through a staggering pile of gifts. For a child newly arrived in the States, colliding with a strange culture is never more bewildering than in that first confrontation with the excesses of an American Christmas. And even in the best of circumstances, family reunions are rarely conflict-free. There may be a *tío* who drinks too much rum, a crazy aunt, an estranged father, obnoxious cousins. And Christmas can be a time of bitter revelation, when adults become too distracted to maintain the facade they normally use to shield a child from grown-up reality.

The stories we received for that holiday issue were threaded together by a string of confusion and misfortune. The authors' reactions to the holiday foibles and sorrows they faced ranged from poignant to hilarious: from Estela Herrera's anguished tale of her pet goat to Jaime Manrique's sardonic account of his aunt's attempted suicide. And there was the sense of wonder, too, the small child's astonished response to the magic of it all.

We realized that the scope of emotions engendered by remembering Christmas past was far more than we could begin to explore in a magazine feature. Esmeralda Santiago and I had become friends through the evolution of *Sí* magazine, and her story led the section that appeared in that holiday issue. Together we began to expand on those memories. This book is the result of our yearlong collaboration.

We invited more authors to contribute memories, and once again we looked for writers with a variety of geographic origins. We invited friends, colleagues, authors whose work we admired, writers we'd always wanted to meet. This time we knew that we could expect to find a commonality of experience that transcended ethnicity. Still, we were stunned by the intensity of many of the pieces we received.

As the stories arrived, we felt as though each writer had sent us a Christmas gift. As we read each one, it was like unwrapping an unexpected present, and we marveled that we were given the privilege of sharing something so intensely personal. The stories were like secrets told to a close friend. "This is what it was like when I was little. This is what my family was like. This is how it seemed to me as a child."

Given the chance to write longer pieces, the authors used Christmas as a springboard to describe experiences common to all people: poverty, alienation, loss of innocence, a child's growing awareness of life's harshness. Gary Soto remembered the meager Christmas of a boy raised on welfare. Michael Nava opened our eyes to the feelings of a child at a charity Christmas party. Julia Alvarez described the moment when the terror of living in a dictatorship first cracked the protective seal of a child's world. When there was humor in the stories, it was often derived from specifically Latino experiences, from the absurdity of clashing cultures—Ilan Stavans's account of latkes with mole in Mexico City, Francisco Goldman's memory of *posadas* in Newton, Massachusetts, Ray Suárez's tale of tropical *aguinaldos* in a frozen Chicago.

And the warmth and joy of the holiday was there, as well. Memories of good food are intrinsically happy—Puerto Rican author Rosario Morales remembers her mother's *asopao* simmering on the stove. Colombian poet Jaime Manrique has not forgotten his family's delicious Christmas *pasteles*. As we read the stories, Esmeralda and I found ourselves hungry for the dishes mentioned. What makes Ilan Stavans's grandmother's *pescado a la veracruzana* so special that he still remembers it years later and thousands of miles from home? Why is Martín Espada's alter ego a wrestler named El Pernil? Would it be too much to ask Ilan to phone Mexico City for that fish recipe? And could Jaime please ask his family what was in those *pasteles*?

From the many foods mentioned in the Christmas memories, Esmeralda and I developed the idea for a pan-Latino holiday banquet, a menu like no other. We called the authors who, in turn, often called their mothers, their sisters, their aunts. We called our own mothers; we called our friends. We consulted cookbooks and compared notes. Then, on two coasts, the cooking began. In Westchester County, New York, Esmeralda's kitchen was fragrant with the aroma of her *arroz con coco*, while two thousand miles away, trays of anise-scented *bizcochitos* were browning in my Los Angeles oven. We tested the recipes, made adjustments, retested.

Finally, we were ready to prepare our Christmas feast. Esmeralda's friend, Laura Cohen, generously agreed to lend us her spacious kitchen. Other friends were enlisted to help with the preparations. Some ingredients were hard to find in Westchester supermarkets, so I shipped two FedEx boxes full of treasures from the ranch market in my L.A. neighborhood: plantain leaves, chiles, *queso blanco*. I tucked bottles of Pico de Gallo powdered chiles and packets of *achiote* paste into my suitcase and got on a plane.

On the morning of the big day, Esmeralda's mother was on call in Florida, in case we got into trouble with any of the Puerto Rican specialties on our menu. The cooking was a party in itself. Eight women stood around the big kitchen table, wrapping tamales in corn husks, folding plantain leaves into *pasteles*—old friends and new friends, mothers and daughters, dogs winding their way among eight sets of legs, patrolling the floor, hoping one of us would drop a bit of stuffing.

In the frenzy of the last hour, we waited our turn at the stove, took turns with the blender, chopped onions and tomatoes like a bunch of crazy samurai. Esmeralda decided that this was the moment to ease the tension with a first round of *coquito*, the lethal Puerto Rican coconut-cream-rum drink. Fathers and brothers, little sisters and assorted friends arrived. All the dishes were tasted, most of them highly praised, some of them requiring a bit of adjustment.

At the end of the evening, when we were too tired to move and too tipsy to care, Esmeralda cranked up the music. The women and girls somehow found the energy to jump up and salsa, while the men looked happily, blearily on.

Outside, the first real snow of the season blanketed the lawns. Christmas would arrive again in a few weeks. Looking around that big room full of people, I felt as though I had stepped into the pages of our book, and I was engulfed in a wave of sentimentality. There were dear old friends with whom I had shared decades of my life, children on the verge of adulthood whom I remembered as bulges in their mothers' bellies, new friends who were like sisters to me now. The room was warm from the blaze in the fireplace and the glow of shared pleasures. I was exhausted and sated, feeling the rum. So, I thought, this is Las Navidades. This is what all the fuss is about.

JOIE DAVIDOW

LAS CHRISTMAS

Aurora Levins Morales

Aurora Levins Morales spent her childhood in Maricao, Puerto Rico. She is coauthor, with her mother, Rosario Morales, of Getting Home Alive *(Firebrand Books), a collection of autobiographical poetry and prose. Her work has been published in* Ms. *magazine,* The American Voice, *and many anthologies. Her most recent books are a collection of essays,* Medicine Stories: History, Culture, and the Politics of Integrity *(South End Press, 1998) and* Remedios: Stories of Earth and Iron from the History of Puertorriqueños *(Beacon, 1998), a prose-poetry retelling of Puerto Rican history through the lives of women. She teaches Puerto Rican history at the University of California, Berkeley, and women's studies at the University of Minnesota, and has homes in both states.*

DULCE DE NARANJA

IN PUERTO RICO, Las Navidades is a season, not a single day. Early in December, with the hurricane season safely over, the thick autumn rains withdraw and sun pours down on the island uninterrupted. This will be a problem by March, when the reservoirs empty, and the shores of Lake Luchetti show wider and wider rings of red mud, until the lake bottom curls up into little pancakes of baked clay and the skeletons of long-drowned houses are revealed. Then, people wait anxiously for rain, pray that the sweet, white coffee blossoms of April don't wither on the branch. But during Navidades, the sun shines on branches heavily laden with hard, green

3

berries starting to ripen and turn red. Oranges glow on the trees, *aguinaldos* start to dominate the airwaves of Radio Café, and women start grating yuca and plantain for *pasteles,* and feeling up the pigs and chickens, calculating the best moment for the slaughter.

It was 1962 or maybe 1965. Any of those years. Barrio Indiera Baja of Maricao and Barrio Rubias of Yauco are among the most remote inhabited places on the island, straddling the crest of the Cordillera Central among the mildewed ruins of old coffee plantations, houses, and sheds left empty when the tides of international commerce withdrew. A century ago, Yauco and Maricao fought bitterly to annex this prime coffee-growing land at a time when Puerto Rican coffee was the best in the world. But Brazil flooded the market with cheaper, faster-growing varieties. There were hurricanes and invasions and the coffee region slid into decline.

In the 1960s of my childhood most people in Indiera still worked in coffee, but everyone was on food stamps except the handful of *hacendados* and young people who kept leaving for town jobs or for New York and Connecticut.

Those were the years of modernization. Something was always being built or inaugurated—dams, bridges, new roads, shopping centers, and acres of housing developments. Helicopters crossed the mountains installing electrical poles in places too inaccessible for trucks (while keeping an eye out for illegal rum stills). During my entire childhood the *acueducto,* the promise of running water, inched its way toward us with much fanfare and very little result. When the pipes were finally in place, the engineers discovered that there was rarely enough pressure to drive the water up the steep slopes north of the reservoir. About once a month the faucets, left open all the time, started to sputter. Someone called out "¡*Acueduuuuucto!*" and everyone ran to fill their buckets before the pipes went dry again.

Navidades was the season for extravagance in the midst of hardship. Food was saved up and then lavishly spread on the table. New clothing was bought in town or made up by a neighbor, and furniture was brought home, to be paid off in installments once the harvest was in.

One of those years, Doña Gina's husband bought her an indoor stove with an oven, and all the neighbors turned out to see. They were going to roast the pig indoors! Not a whole pig, of course, but I was there watching when Don

Lencho slashed the shaved skin and rubbed the wounds with handfuls of mashed garlic and fresh oregano, *achiote* oil and vinegar, black pepper and salt. Doña Gina was making *arroz con dulce*, tray after tray of cinnamon-scented rice pudding with coconut. The smells kept all the children circling around the kitchen like hungry sharks.

This was before every house big enough for a chair had sprouted a TV antenna. My brother and I went down to the Canabal house to watch occasional episodes of *Bonanza* dubbed into Spanish: I liked to watch the lips move out of sync with the voice that said, "*Vámonos, Hoss!*" And by 1966 there would be a TV in the seventh-grade classroom at Arturo Lluberas Junior High, down near Yauco, where the older girls would crowd in to watch *El Show del Mediodía*. But in Indiera and Rubias nobody was hooked on TV Christmas specials yet, so when the season began, people still tuned up their *cuatros* and guitars, took down the *güiros* and maracas and started going house to house looking for free drinks. So while Don Lencho kept opening the oven to baste the pig, Chago and Nestor and Papo played *aguinaldos* and *plenas* and Carmencita improvised lyrics back and forth with Papo, each trying to top the other in witty commentary, the guests hooting and clapping when one or the other scored a hit. No one talked much about Cheíto and Luis away in Vietnam, or Adita's fiancé running off with a pregnant high-school girl a week before the wedding or Don Toño coughing up blood all the time. "*Gracias a Dios*," said Doña Gina, "*aquí estamos*."

During Navidades the cars of city relatives started showing up parked in the road next to the red and green jeeps. My girlfriends had to stay close to home and wear starched dresses, and the boys looked unnaturally solemn in ironed white shirts, with their hair slicked down. Our relatives were mostly in New York, but sometimes a visitor came all that way, announced ahead of time by letter, or, now and then, adventurous enough to try finding our farm with just a smattering of Spanish and a piece of paper with our names.

The neighbors grew their own *gandules* and plantain, but, except for a few vegetables, we didn't farm our land. My father drove to San Juan every week to teach at the university and did most of our shopping there, at the Pueblo supermarket on the way out of town. Sometimes all those overflowing bags of groceries weighed on my conscience, especially when I went to the store with my best friend, Tata, and waited while she asked Don Paco to put another meager pound of rice on their tab. My father was a biologist and a commuter. This was how we got our frozen blintzes and English muffins, fancy cookies and date-nut bread.

But during Navidades it seemed, for a little while, as if everyone had enough. My father brought home Spanish *turrón*—sticky white nougat full of almonds, wrapped in thin edible layers of papery white stuff. The best kind is the hard *turrón* you have to break with a hammer. Then there were all the gooey, intensely sweet fruit-pastes you ate with crumbly white cheese. The dense, red-brown *guayaba*; golden mango; sugar-crusted, pale brown *batata*; and dazzlingly white coconut. And my favorite, *dulce de naranja,* a tantalizing mix of bitter orange and sugar, the alternating tastes always startling on the tongue. We didn't eat pork, but my father cooked canned corned beef with raisins and onions and was the best Jewish *tostón* maker in the world.

Christmas trees were still a strange gringo custom for most of our neighbors, but each year we picked something to decorate, this household of transplanted New Yorkers—my Puerto Rican mother, my Jewish father, and the two, then three of us, "*americanitos*" growing up like wild *guayabas* on an overgrown and half-abandoned coffee farm. One year we cut a miniature grove of bamboo and folded dozens of tiny origami cranes in gold and silver paper to hang on the branches. Another year it was the tightly rolled, flame-red flowers of *señorita* with traditional, shiny Christmas balls glowing among the lush green foliage. Sometimes it was boughs of Australian pine hung with old ornaments we brought with us from New York in 1960, those pearly ones with the inverted cones carved into their sides like funnels of fluted, silver and gold light.

The only telephone was the one at the crossroads, which rarely worked, so other than my father's weekly trip to San Juan, the mail was our only link with the world outside the barrio. Every day during Las Navidades, when my brother and I would stop at the crossroads for the mail, there would be square envelopes in bright colors bringing Season's Greetings from faraway people we'd never met. But there were also packages. We had one serious sweet tooth on each side of the family. Every year my Jewish grandmother sent metal tins full of brightly wrapped toffee in iridescent paper that my brother and I saved for weeks. Every year my Puerto Rican grandfather sent boxes of Jordan almonds in sugary pastel colors and jumbo packages of Hershey's Kisses and Tootsie Rolls.

Of course this was also the season of rum, of careening jeeploads of festive people in constant motion up and down the narrow twisting roads of the mountains. You could hear the laughter and loud voices fade and blare as they wound in and out of the curves. All along the sides of the roads there were shrines—white crosses or painted rocks with artificial flowers and the dates of horrible accidents: head-on collisions when two jeeps held onto the crown of the road too long; places where drivers mistook the direction of the next dark curve and rammed into a tree or plummeted, arcing into the air and over the dizzying edge, to crash among the broken branches of citrus and *pomarrosa* and leaving a wake of destruction. Some of those ravines still held the rusted frames of old trucks and cars no one knew how to retrieve after the bodies were taken home for burial.

It was rum, the year my best friend's father died. Early Navidades, just coming into December, and parties already in full swing. Chiqui, Tata, Chinita, and I spent a lot of time out in the road, while inside, women in black dresses prayed, cleaned, and cooked. Every so often one of them would come out on the porch and call Tata or Chiqui, who were cousins, to get something from the store or go down the hill to the spring to fetch more buckets of water.

No one in Indiera was called by their real name. It was only in school, when the teacher took attendance, that you found out all those Tatas and Titas, Papos and Juniors were named Milagros and Carmen María, José Luis and Dionisio. The few names people used became soft and blurred in our mouths, in the country–Puerto Rican Spanish we inherited from Andalucian immigrants who had settled in those hills centuries ago and kept as far as they could from church and state alike. We mixed *yanqui* slang with the archaic accents of the sixteenth century, so that Ricardo became Hicaldo while Wilson turned into Güilsong. In the 1960s, every morning the radio still announced all the saints whose names could be given to children born that day, which is presumably how people ended up with names like Migdonio, Eduvigis, and Idelfonso.

Anyway, Tata's father was dying of alcoholism, his liver finally surrendering to forty or fifty years of heavy drinking and perhaps his heart collapsing under the weight of all the beatings and abuse he had dished out to his wife and fourteen children. Tata was his youngest child—ten, scrawny, fast on her feet. Her city nieces and nephews were older, but in the solemn days of waiting for death, she played her status for all it was worth, scolding them for laughing or playing, reminding them that she was their aunt, and must be respected. All day the women swept and washed and cooked and in the heat of the afternoon sat sipping coffee, talking softly on the porch.

In our classroom, where we also awaited news of the death, we were deep into the usual holiday rituals of public school. The girls cut out poinsettia flowers from red construction paper and the boys got to climb on chairs to help Meesee Torres hang garishly colored pictures of the Three Kings above the blackboard. We practiced singing "*Alegría, alegría, alegría,*" and during Spanish class we read stories of miraculous generosity and goodwill.

Late one Tuesday afternoon after school, we heard the wailing break out across the road, and the next day Meesee Torres made us all line up and walk up the hill to Tata's house to pay our respects. We filed into their living room, past the open coffin, and each of us placed a single flower in the vase Meesee had brought, then filed out again. What astonished me was how small Don Miguel looked, nested in white satin, just a little brown man without those bulging veins of rage at his temples and the heavy hands waiting to hit.

The next night the *velorio* began. The road was full of jeeps and city cars, and more dressed-up relatives than ever before spilled out of the little house. For three days people ate and drank and prayed and partied, laughing and chatting, catching up on old gossip and rekindling ancient family arguments. Now and then someone would have to separate a couple of drunk men preparing to hit out with fists. Several of the women had *ataques*, falling to the ground and tearing their hair and clothing.

The first night of the *velorio* was also the first night of Hanukkah that year. While Tata went to church with her mother to take part in *rosarios* and novenas and Catholic mysteries I knew nothing about, my family sat in the darkened living room of our house and lit the first candle on the menorah, the one that lights all the others. Gathered around that small glow, my father told the story of the Maccabees who fought off an invading empire, while, across the road, Tata's family laughed together, making life bigger than death. I remember sitting around the candles, thinking of those ancient Jews hanging in for thirty years to take back their temple, what it took to not give up; and of all the women in the barrio raising children who sometimes died and you never knew who would make it and who wouldn't, of people setting off for home and maybe meeting death in another jeep along the way. And in the middle of a bad year, a year of too much loss, there were still two big pots of *pasteles* and a house full of music and friends. Life, like the *acueducto*, seemed to be unpredictable, maddening, and sometimes startlingly abundant.

That night I lay awake for a long time in the dark, listening to life walking toward me. Luís would never come home from Vietnam or would come home crazy, but the war would end someday and most of us would grow up. My father would be fired from the university for protesting that war, and we would be propelled into a new life, but I would find lifelong friends and new visions for myself in an undreamed-of city. Death and celebration, darkness and light, the miraculous star of the Three Kings and the miracle of a lamp burning for eight days on just a drop of oil. So much uncertainty and danger and so much stubborn faith. And somewhere out there in the dark, beyond the voices of Tata's family still murmuring across the road, the three wise mysterious travelers were already making their way to me, carrying something unknown, precious, strange.

Puerto Rican Tostones con Mojito

❧ FRIED PLANTAINS

Tostones are served year-round in Puerto Rico, where no party is complete without them. Traditionally, they are pressed with the heel of the hand; modern cooks can find wooden *tostoneras* in Latin American groceries—or even at the San Juan airport.

4 cups water for soaking
6 green plantains

oil for frying
4 tablespoons salt

Add 2 tablespoons salt to 2 cups water. Set aside. Peel plantains. Cut in rounds about 1 1/2 inches wide. Place slices in salted water for ten minutes. Drain.

Heat 2 inches of oil in a deep frying pan. The oil should be hot but not smoking.

Place plantain slices on a slotted spoon and dip into the hot oil. Fry over moderate heat until plantains are soft, about 8 minutes.

Remove slices from the pan with the slotted spoon onto paper towels. Allow to drain and cool slightly.

Press fried slices between sheets of waxed paper using a rolling pin or use a *tostonera*. The slices should be about 1/2 inch thick when pressed. The thinner you press them, the crispier they'll become.

Make a fresh batch of salt water, again using 2 tablespoons of salt to 2 cups of water. Dip fried pressed slices in fresh salted water quickly, remove and drain.

Fry again, about 5 minutes, or until crispy.

Remove with slotted spoon to paper towels and drain again.

Serve warm, salted, plain or with *mojito*.

Makes 20 to 30 tostones, depending on the size of the plantains

MOJITO (OPTIONAL)

4 garlic cloves, crushed into a paste   *salt and pepper to taste*
¼ cup olive oil

Combine ingredients. Use as a dip.

Junot Díaz

*Junot Díaz was born and raised in Santo Domingo, the Dominican Republic.
His story collection,* Drown, *was published in English by Riverhead Books, and
in Spanish (under the title* Negocios*) by Vintage Español. His work has appeared
in* The New Yorker, Best American Fiction, Story, *and* The Paris Review.

THE THREE KINGS LOSE THEIR WAY

I DON'T REMEMBER WELL my first Christmas in the States.
My family left Santo Domingo in mid-December. I was seven that
year and vaguely recall celebrating Three Kings Day early, perhaps
even on the day of our departure from the island. My mom wasn't leaving
anything up to chance; she'd rather us children celebrate our holiday weeks
early in Santo Domingo, our home, than save it for a land she did not know
and did not, instinctively, trust. I remember receiving a plastic canteen, a tin
top, and a plastic machine gun, none of which survived more than a month in
the States. The machine gun might even have been my brother's. He was
older, and I'd never known him to have much interest in toys—he was in the
habit of passing all his shit to me or my little sister.

My green card dutifully reports that I arrived at Kennedy Airport on the
eleventh of December with the rest of my family. I am scowling in my green-
card picture, a small serious boy who, in an effort to please his military father,
buttoned all his shirts to the top. My attempt to ingratiate myself with my
pops is not as important as my expression: Although the photo was snapped

in a backroom studio in Santo Domingo, it best predicted what I would feel like when, upon debarking from the plane, I experienced a New York winter for the first time in my life. The December winds plowed me open. We didn't even have coats and wouldn't have them until we reached our apartment in New Jersey. My father had forgotten to bring them to the airport—and where the hell would my family have found them in Santo Domingo?

I remember my first weeks in the States as a series of astonishments: the cold, my father, English, our apartment, the indoor plumbing, the TV, the loneliness of apartment life, of being a recently arrived immigrant. I not only had to acclimate myself to our new surroundings, but also to my father's presence. He was a man I'd previously only heard stories about. But now he was with us, an intense, complicated presence.

In those first weeks, Christmas must have been everywhere around us— on the TV, on the radio, in the stores where we shopped for the socks and toothbrushes our family would need in order to become like *los americanos* (a metamorphosis my father regarded very seriously). I suspect I took it for granted that this was what the United States was about, that all the colors, the clamor, and the decorations were part of every day, that stores were always flooded with waves of anxious, frantic, irritated customers. I was overwhelmed by it all. As for the much-anticipated snow, we saw a lot of it on the television, a bewildering, accumulating whiteness, but we wouldn't have any in our part of the state until late the next month. On the twenty-second of December, my brother and I watched through a window while a neighbor in the next building rigged his porch with beautiful strings of Christmas lights. We lived across from Mr. Polanca for twenty years, and he never once changed his routine. The brother was like clockwork. The tree went up on the twentieth, the lights on the twenty-second. And it all came down on the seventh of January.

That year, Christmas came and went. I remember plenty of things from those first weeks but not that day specifically. I remember sneaking out of the apartment one night, while my parents were sleeping, to check out everybody's lights in the neighborhood; I remember that my brother and I got lost, and it took us nearly three freezing hours to find our way back to our apartment in the dark. I remember my birthday on the thirty-first of December and the flimsy Hess trucks my father brought us for Three Kings Day, but I don't remember Christmas. I must have been too caught up in my adaptations to take much notice. The next year would be a different story. By then, my siblings and I would speak English. No longer Nabokov's dreaded monolinguists, ours would be mongrel tongues. We'd also have enough "American" culture inside of us to accord the appropriate amount of approbation to the holiday of Christmas. It would never again slip by unnoticed, but Three Kings Day would, which says a lot more about what we lost in coming to the States, I think, than about what we gained.

Mandalit del Barco

Mandalit del Barco was born in Lima, Peru and grew up in Baldwin, Kansas. She is a frequently heard staff reporter for National Public Radio. She is also a contributor to the NPR program Latino USA. *A former staff writer for the* Miami Herald, *she is a past contributor to* The Village Voice.

PEMEX XMAS

 SINCE WE WERE the only Peruvian-Mexican family in the one-horse town of Baldwin, Kansas, we invented our own multicultural rituals to celebrate Christmas del Barco.

It was the 1960s, and we had immigrated from South America to the Sunflower State, where Mom had grown up. While in Peru studying folklore on a Fulbright scholarship, Mom met Dad, a dashing journalist and actor—and their international love story began. I came into the picture in cosmopolitan Lima, and eighteen months later we moved to Kansas, just before my brother, Andy, was born.

In the years that followed, Mom taught Spanish literature at a small college while Dad worked on a graduate thesis in anthropology. We were probably the only family in Baldwin who collectively protested the war in Vietnam and boycotted nonunion grapes. While our neighbors remained nestled comfortably in some earlier, small-town era—a throwback to the fifties, forties or even the thirties—we campaigned against Nixon, championed women's lib, and joined in Native American powwows. The place always reminded me of *Mayberry, R.F.D.*, though Andy jokes that if Baldwin was Mayberry, then we were something like the Addams Family. Let's just say I had the feeling we were *not* in Lima anymore.

In this snowbound prairie town, our hybrid holiday would always begin with the perennial viewing of our TV favorite, *How the Grinch Stole Christmas*. Instead of "roast beast," our meal generally consisted of Peruvian *papas a la huancaína* and a delicious *marisco*-filled *chupe de camarones* made by Dad, who pointed out that in Quechua—the Indian language of his native Peru—*chupe* means soup. Sometimes he'd make ceviche, or Mom would prepare tamales and enchiladas. For dessert, we savored the *buñuelos y chocolate*, which Mom made in her traditional Mexican style, spicing the condensed milk and Hershey's with sticks of cinnamon.

On Christmas Eve, Andy and I would inevitably fall asleep waiting for our pet cats to talk to us, as we were told all the animals would at midnight. Was that a Mexican tradition? Peruvian? American? Our ideas about Christmas were *una mezcla*, a mix. Among the figurines in our *nacimiento*, the Nativity scene handmade in Ayacucho out of *piedra de Huamanga* (an alabaster from the Andean highlands), Andy and I would position our Sesame Street finger puppets. This way, Big Bird, Grover, Ernie, and Bert—whom we dressed in red felt costumes—assumed their rightful places next to Baby Jesus and a fuzzy llama, scaled to size.

Mom and Dad would address our gifts with joke tags like "For Andy: from the third elf on the left," or "For Mandalit: from the combined elf chorus." In return, Andy and I would put on yet another ad-libbed puppet show, from behind the cleverly designed puppet theater Dad built for us. Or we'd make up another satirical radio play, recorded reel-to-reel, using *Mad* magazine–style puns, like this feminist Christmas comedy in which Ms. Sandy Claus takes over the job of delivering toys one year when Santa is sick. She's been caught breaking and entering and is now standing trial.

ANDY (*as thief Rob Burr, with a Brooklyn accent*): I was goin' ta work on my regular block, and I sees dis here dude widdah red suit. I figured he wuz tryin' ta muscle in on my act. Then as he was goin' tru the window, his beard got caught on a tree limb and came off. I sees dat it was a lady, of all tings. I figuredat she was what you might call one of dem male impersonators.

MANDALIT (*as militant defendant Sandy Claus*): How dare you insult my identity!

ANDY (*this time as stuffy Judge Soy Bean*): Order!

MANDALIT (*now a sarcastic trial watcher*): I'll take a pastrami on rye . . .

Besides creating satires, my family introduced the neighborhood to some Latino traditions. Folks in Baldwin didn't know from *las posadas*—caroling in Spanish—and there was no *misa del gallo*—midnight mass. But we'd invite the Brady Bunch–like neighborhood kids to help us light candles in the sidewalk *luminarias* we made from paper lunch bags weighted with sand (a New Mexico tradition from Mom's side). And they helped us knock down our homemade piñatas. Somehow, we even taught them a few Mexican and Peruvian folk songs, though they probably had no idea what the words meant. But that didn't matter much.

There was always a foreign student or five visiting our house for Christmas—from Peru or Kenya or China or Costa Rica. Imported from Somalia, Mexico, and Colombia, too. One year, the entire college soccer team showed up to share in our polyglot celebrations. We were all expatriates, living in the land of Ahs, making things up as we went along.

Feliz Navidad. Or as they say in Kansas, Merry Christmas.

RUEDA, RUEDA

A Villancico from Peru

Rueda, rueda por la montaña
Blanca luz de sol.

Rueda, rueda la buena nueva
Que nació el Redentor.

Rueda, rueda la buena nueva
Que Él ya nació.

Roll, roll down the mountain,
White light of the sun.

Roll, roll the good news
That the Redeemer is born.

Roll, roll the good news,
That He is born.

Papas a la Huancaína

PERUVIAN POTATO SALAD

There are two versions of this recipe. This one uses *salsa cruda,* an uncooked sauce. Some families prefer a *salsa cocida,* a sauce cooked on the stove, and add crushed Saltines, peanuts, and other ingredients. This is a home recipe contributed by Mandalit's parents, Dolores and Renán del Barco, so feel free to add or subtract garnishes as you like.

THE POTATOES

10 yellow potatoes

Boil the potatoes in salted water just until they can be pierced easily with a fork. Don't overcook! They shouldn't be mushy. Cool and peel.

THE SAUCE

1 cup finely minced white onion
hot salted water for soaking
2 cups queso blanco *or French feta cheese*
4 hard-boiled egg yolks
2 tablespoons ground, dried jalapeños, or 2 whole fresh jalapeño peppers, seeded, chopped and lightly fried

salt and pepper
1 cup salad oil
1 cup evaporated milk (or cream if your diet can take it)
¼ cup fresh lime juice, or to taste

Soak the sliced white onion in hot salted water.

Mash the cheese and egg yolks together in an electric mixer or blender. Add jalapeño peppers, salt, and pepper. Mix well. Add oil, pouring gradually, while continuing to mix on high speed. Add milk and lime juice, blending well. Drain the white onion well, and fold into the mixture with a spoon.

THE GARNISH

thinly sliced red onion	*1 or 2 small ears of sweet corn*
hot water for soaking	*(cooked and cut into small*
lime juice	*sections)*
pinch of crushed red chiles	*pitted ripe olives*
1 to 2 heads butter lettuce	*5 hard-boiled eggs, sliced*

Rinse the sliced red onion in hot water, then cover with lime juice and chiles.

Slice the peeled potatoes. Arrange butter lettuce leaves around the edge of a serving platter. Pile sliced potatoes in the center and cover with the sauce. Decorate with corn, olives, sliced boiled eggs, and the drained red onion rings.

Makes 8 servings

Gustavo Pérez Firmat

Gustavo Pérez Firmat was born in Havana, Cuba, and raised in Miami, Florida. A recipient of fellowships from the National Endowment for the Humanities, the American Council of Learned Societies, and the Guggenheim Foundation, he is currently Professor of Spanish at Duke University. His numerous volumes of literary and cultural criticism include Literature and Liminality *and* Do the Americas Have a Common Literature? *(both Duke University Press) and* Life on the Hyphen: The Cuban-American Way *(University of Texas Press), which was awarded the Eugene M. Kayden University Press National Book Award. His collections of poetry in Spanish and English include* Carolina Cuban, Equivocaciones, *and* Bilingual Blues. *This story is adapted from a chapter of his memoir,* Next Year in Cuba: A Cubano's Coming of Age in America *(Anchor Books).*

GOOD NIGHT TO NOCHEBUENA

WHEN I WAS GROWING up in Cuba, Nochebuena—literally, "the good night"—was the holiest and happiest night of the year. Divided in half by midnight mass, the Cuban Christmas Eve oscillated, sharply but predictably, between the sacred and the profane, between religious ritual and secular mirth-making. Since, in the fifties, Catholics were still required to fast before receiving Holy Communion, the celebration that accompanied the religious observance was not supposed to begin until one or

two o'clock in the morning, after everyone got back from *la misa del gallo*, whose name goes back to the Roman custom of holding mass at dawn, when the *gallos*, or cocks, crowed. But cultural differences being what they are, Cuban roosters began crowing long before the Roman cocks. Well before midnight my uncles, who typically were less devout than their wives, were already well into their Bacardi cups. When they accompanied their wives and children to midnight mass, they remained on the steps of the church while the rest of us went inside to pray. It was a curious sight: from inside the church I could see the crowd of men, impeccably dressed in their long-sleeved guayaberas with bow ties, milling around and talking. The hubbub was such that Father Spirali, the Italian-born pastor of the San Agustín parish in Havana, sometimes had to interrupt the mass to hush the men congregated outside. I couldn't wait to be old enough to join them.

Nochebuena was essentially a feast for grown-ups. Because most Cuban children received their holiday gifts on January 6, the Feast of the Epiphany, nothing that happened on Christmas Eve had to do directly with us. At our house my brothers, my baby sister, and I had to go to sleep before *la misa del gallo*. The last couple of years in Cuba, my brother Pepe and I were allowed to attend midnight mass, but since our American-tinged household was visited both by Santa Claus and the Three Wise Men (Santa brought the better gifts), we were still packed off to bed sooner rather than later with the pretext that Santa wouldn't come until all of the children were asleep. But it was hard to get to sleep on Nochebuena, a good but not a silent night.

At least for me, the best part of Christmas wasn't Nochebuena but the preparations that preceded it. Like other Cuban couples, my parents had an uneven division of festive labor: my mother prepared, and my father partied. Her job was to set everything up; his job was to make the most of her arrangements, for the benefit of others as well as himself. If he was the life of the party, she was its machinery. Her preparations for Nochebuena began in early December with the arrival of boxes of Spanish nougat, marzipan, filberts, sparkling wines, and other holiday staples—gifts from the people my father did business with. We'd buy the tallest Christmas tree available at the American-style supermarket and then spend several afternoons putting up the ornaments and setting up the Nativity scene. The fake fireplace in the living room, which was just the right size for the large plaster figures of Baby

Jesus, Mary, and Joseph, made a marvelous manger. Under the tree we built a replica of Bethlehem, complete with river, bridge, shepherds, and sheep. Off to one side, somewhat in the distance, the Three Wise Men approached on their camels, bearing gifts. In the foyer my mother placed mirrors and cotton swatches to simulate snow and a frozen lake, which she surrounded with little cottages with red roofs and lights inside. Between early December and the second week in January, this incongruous wintry landscape was the first thing one saw as one entered our Havana home, where even the walls were painted a leafy green.

The puny imported pines that reached the supermarket where we shopped looked like malnourished imitations of the bushy Carolina balsams I later became accustomed to in the States. They shed needles like rain, and no amount of watering could cure their wan, skeletal look. But to us they were incomparably beautiful. Other kids in the neighborhood, whose parents didn't put up Christmas trees, came to our house for awed stares. The point was not the tree, anyway, but the decorations, whose abundance more than made up for the gaping holes in the foliage. Because Americans think of Christmas trees as natural objects (and with good reason: they can see them growing), often their idea of decoration is a red ribbon with a pine cone or some paper cutouts that their kids bring home from school. For us, Christmas trees were exotic imported artifacts that provided an opportunity to demonstrate once again the triumph of man over nature, so we smothered them with decorations: blinking lights, endless rosaries of shiny marble-sized balls, and box upon box of ornaments, including some odd ones like a blown-crystal *bohío* (thatched hut). We buried any residual holes under a canopy of *lágrimas*, literally "tears" but in fact tinsel. Tears blanketed our sagging tree like kudzu weeds. The crowning touch was a large, brightly-lit figure of the Archangel Gabriel, who presided over the living room with arms outstretched. My father got up on a ladder and, tottering above my mother's watchful eye, skewered the angel onto the tree. By the time we were through, several days after we had begun, our formerly spindly tree looked splendid—an anorexic wrapped in jewelry and furs, and with an angelic tiara to boot.

When my family arrived in the United States in October 1960, we stopped celebrating Nochebuena. It seemed pointless to observe this feast in exile, with our unsettled political situation and the family scattered all over—

some relatives still in Cuba and others in New York or Puerto Rico. That first Christmas in Miami we put up a tree, a smaller and greener one, but the only crèche we could afford was a cardboard stable with fold-out figures. Instead of Nochebuena dinner, we had Christmas lunch; instead of the traditional roasted pig, my mother baked a turkey. Sitting around the table on Christmas Day, we weren't so much gloomy as dazed. We had been living in this house only a few weeks, everything was topsy-turvy, it wasn't clear what we were supposed to think or say. There we were, just my parents and their four children around the table, suddenly reduced to an American nuclear family. Earlier that morning Santa had left gifts for those of us who still believed in him, but two weeks later the Three Wise Men didn't show up. I remember hearing my mother tell my little sister that Melchior, Gaspar, and Balthasar had stayed in Cuba.

By the late sixties almost everybody in our immediate family had left Cuba, and even if they didn't live in Miami they were still near enough to come down for Christmas. Since we were all together again, it no longer felt inappropriate to celebrate this feast in exile. Indeed, the opposite thing happened: distance from the homeland made us celebrate the occasion all the more vigorously, for Nochebuena became one of the ways of holding on to Cuba. Although the celebrations were less splendid than the old ones, the essentials remained the same. During those years Little Havana was already full of Cuban markets that carried all the typical foods; and if a family didn't have the time or the skill to roast a pig in the backyard, a pig already cooked could be bought at the corner bodega, along with containers of *congrí* and yuca.

Like the food, the faces in our family gathering hadn't changed much. Our Miami Nochebuenas included many of the same relatives that had attended the gatherings in Cuba. Tío Mike always arrived early to set up what he called his "intellectual laboratory," where he concocted mysterious martinis by looking up the proportions in one of his pocket notebooks. While Mike experimented, his wife, Mary, minced around in her gold high-heeled thongs with the furred straps. Tony, an uncle who had been a cabaret singer in Havana and was now a waiter in New York, crooned boleros accompanied by my sister on the guitar, while my father danced randy rumbas with any willing (and sometimes unwilling) partner. At some point during the evening, with eyes sparkling from a glass or two of *sidra,* my Castilian grandmother did her famous jota, which was followed by the ritual paso doble with my father.

But even if we went to church, pigged out on roast pork, and drank and danced, these lively parties weren't really clones of the Cuban Nochebuenas. Without anyone being overly aware of it, the Cuban Nochebuena and the American Christmas had started to get acquainted, to negotiate a compromise. Not only was Christmas sneaking up on Nochebuena; Nochebuena was converging on Christmas. Like my grandmother doing the jota next to the Christmas tree, Cuban customs had begun to marry American ways.

On the face of it, the marriage was not an easy one. As an eager anticipation of the birth of Christ, Nochebuena has a high-strung, restive feel. Many Cubans spend the night in perpetual motion, going from one house to the next, a custom that supposedly goes back to the biblical story of Mary and Joseph wandering around Bethlehem looking for a place to spend the night. On the evening of December 24 we divide into two camps: the squatters and the roamers. The squatters stay put, cook, stock plenty of drinks, and keep their doors open. The roamers make the rounds. Since we were always squatters, part of the fun of Nochebuena was having people show up at our doorstep at any hour of the night, have a couple of drinks, eat, dance, and then move on to the next house. Needless to say, it's safer to squat than to roam, but it's the roamers who give the evening that extra burst of *embullo,* that extra hit of festive fuel.

By contrast, the spirit of Christmas is neither raucous nor nomadic. As befits a family holiday, Christmas is merry but not moveable, joyful but not extravagant. Whereas Nochebuena is a nocturnal feast, Christmas is a daytime celebration, a holiday in the full sense of the word. If Nochebuena is all motion and commotion, Christmas is peace. On Christmas, families gather to exchange gifts and spend time together, not to hoot and howl. Children are a big part of Christmas, but during Nochebuena they are little more than a nuisance. Our Nochebuena photographs show bunches of grown-ups living it up; our Christmas photographs picture parents and children gathered around the tree. When Christmas encounters Nochebuena, Cuban nights run into American days.

In our house the marriage of day and night occurred when my siblings and cousins and I grew up and began to have children of our own. By the midseventies and for several years thereafter we had achieved a rough balance between the "Cuban" and the "American" ends of the family. The older Cubans, mostly men like my father and my uncles, celebrated Nochebuena; their American-born grandchildren did the same for Christmas. As a member of the intermediate generation, I swung back and forth between one and the other, sometimes playing Cuban son to my father and at other times playing American dad to my son. During these balanced years, the prospect of Christmas morning made Nochebuena a little more sedate, and Nochebuena made Christmas a little more lively. Since the adults had to be up at the crack of dawn to open presents with the kids, we couldn't stay up all night and then go for breakfast to La Carreta or Versailles. Besides, the house was too small for the kids to be able to sleep while the adults carried on outside. Since by the 1970s the Church had slackened its rules on fasting, most years dinner was served before midnight mass. By two or three in the morning Nochebuena was over.

I loved these hybrid celebrations, half day and half night, for they seemed to combine the best of both worlds. But, sadly, biculturalism is a balancing act that topples with the generations, and by the end of our third decade in exile our Nochebuenas had changed again. Many of the older members of the family passed away in the 1970s and 1980s; other aunts and uncles were either too old to travel to Miami every December, or too infirm to leave their houses. When his wife died, my uncle Pedro stopped celebrating holidays altogether. (Now he gets on a plane on the morning of December 24 and spends Christmas Eve at the blackjack tables in the Bahamas; a *noche buena* is when he doesn't lose too much money.) Then also, those in my generation have their own lives and can't always make it down to Miami for Christmas. Once every few years, some of us still coincide in Miami for Nochebuena, but it seems to happen less and less often. With the death of the old-timers, Cuba is dying too.

Every Nochebuena for the last several years my mother grumbles that this will be her last—that she's getting too old for all of the preparations—but come the following year she roasts another leg of pork, cooks another pot of *congrí*, and tries to get the family together. However Americanized she may say she is, she doesn't seem willing to give up this Cuban custom. Old Havanas are hard to break, but for Nena and Gustavo, Nochebuena has become a mournful holiday, a reminder of how much things have changed in their lives. Years ago Nochebuena used to be a time to remember and celebrate things Cuban. The ritual toast, "Next year in Cuba," set the mood for the evening, a mood both nostalgic and hopeful, for the Nochebuenas of yesteryear were a warrant on the Nochebuenas of tomorrow. During those very good nights, everything harked back to Cuba—the celebrants, the food, the music, the customs. At no other time of the year did Cuba seem so close, did *regreso* seem so imminent. Every year we heard my father's favorite chanteuse, Olga Guillot, singing "White Christmas" with Spanish lyrics. Every year we danced to "La Mora," an old Cuban song whose questioning refrain was uncannily relevant, "*¿Cuándo volverá, La Nochebuena, cuándo volverá?*" "When will it return, Nochebuena, when will it return?" Soon, we all thought, very soon. It turned out not to be so.

In all the years I have resided away from Miami, I've missed only one Nochebuena, and that because one year we decided to spend Christmas at our own home in North Carolina, an experiment that didn't turn out well and won't be repeated. As long as my parents are alive and willing, I'll go to their house for Nochebuena. Although the celebration and the celebrants have changed a great deal through the years, more than I and they would have liked, Nochebuena remains for me the holiest—if no longer the happiest—night of the year.

But I have no illusions. Our Miami Nochebuenas have come to resemble those skeletal Christmas trees from Cuba. I could make a joke and say that you can't make roast pig from a sow's ear, but this is no joke. After my parents have passed away, I hope not until many years from now, I will celebrate Nochebuena in Chapel Hill with my American wife and my almost-American children. Instead of going to Miami, I'll be staying put. I'll be a squatter, not a roamer. But I will be squatting far from home. I know that in Chapel Hill my Nochebuena traditions will suffer a further attenuation, and when this happens I'll find myself in the position that my father occupies now—I will be the only Cuban rooster in the house. The good night, which became less than good in Miami, may well become not good enough in Chapel Hill. My reluctant but hopeful wager is that the not-so-*buena* Nochebuena will be followed by an excellent Christmas.

Cuban Congrí

RICE AND BEANS

3 tablespoons olive oil

3 strips of bacon, each sliced into
    8 small pieces

6 ounces pre-cooked, smoked ham

$1/2$ cup sofrito (recipe on page 32)

2 cloves garlic, crushed into a paste

$1/4$ cup tomato paste

liquid from beans plus enough water
    to make 3 cups

1 teaspoon vinegar

1 bay leaf cut in half

$3/4$ teaspoon cumin powder, or
    $3/4$ teaspoon cumin seed,
    crushed

1 heaping teaspoon fresh oregano, or
    $1/4$ teaspoon powdered oregano

$2^1/2$ teaspoons salt

2 cups short- or medium-grain rice,
    washed and drained

1-pound can of black beans
    (frijoles negros)

Heat the olive oil in a large heavy pot. Fry the bacon over medium-high heat until golden. Remove bacon and drain on paper towels. Set aside.

In the olive oil/bacon grease, fry the ham until well heated and crispy. Remove the ham and set aside.

Lower heat to moderate. Add *sofrito*, garlic paste, and tomato paste. Cook for 3 minutes, stirring frequently.

Raise flame to high and add the liquid from beans, the vinegar, bay leaf, cumin, oregano, and salt. When boiling, add rice and beans. Stir to mix well.

When it boils again, lower flame to moderate and cook uncovered until somewhat dry.

Reduce flame to low, add half the reserved ham cubes, and stir into rice. Cover and cook for 15 minutes.

Stir rice again, cover, and cook another 15 minutes, or until rice is tender.

Serve hot, decorated with the rest of the ham pieces and the fried bacon. For more flavor, stir in 2 tablespoons of extra-virgin olive oil before serving.

Makes 6 servings

SOFRITO

1 onion, peeled

1 medium green bell pepper, seeded

3 sweet chili peppers, seeded

1 tablespoon fresh cilantro

4 cloves garlic

$\frac{1}{2}$ teaspoon dried oregano

Whir all ingredients for the *sofrito* in a blender until chopped. Store in the refrigerator in a tight-lidded container.

Denise Chávez

Denise Chávez is a native of Las Cruces, New Mexico. Her novel, Face of an Angel *(Farrar, Straus and Giroux), was awarded the 1994 Premio Aztlán and the 1995 American Book Award. She is also the author of* The Last of the Menu Girls, *a collection of interrelated short stories. Her forthcoming novel,* Loving Pedro Infante, *will be published by Farrar, Straus and Giroux. A performance artist as well as a writer, Chávez tours in her one-woman show,* Women in the State of Grace, *throughout the United States. She has been the Artistic Director of the Border Book Festival, based in Las Cruces, since its inception in 1994.*

BIG CALZONES

In memory of my parents,
Delfina Rede Chávez and E. E. "Chano" Chávez

IT WAS A TRADITION in our family that each year one of us was presented with an unusual gift: an enormous pair of the biggest, whitest, stretchiest polyester panties you have ever seen, size queen-ultra-mega-4X, clownish, enormous drawers. Just to look at them made you laugh out loud. Mother bought them at Aaronson Brothers Clothing store on Main Street, in our little hometown of Las Cruces, New Mexico. Each year, she wrapped this huge pair of *calzones* in the loveliest paper, tied with an elaborate bow, and gave them to some unsuspecting but delighted

soul in our immediate family. The package was opened to squeals of laughter. You never knew when it would be your turn to receive the panties.

Mother's sense of humor was legendary—and sometimes diabolical. Despite her propriety as a teacher and single mother, she had a great sense of the ridiculous and liked to take photographs of people in disarray. She often ambushed my sister or me in the bathroom—a towel draped loosely around a naked body seated on the toilet, hair in curlers, reading the *National Enquirer*. She kept an album of crazy photographs that I still treasure today.

The first year, I was the one who received the big *calzones*. As I opened the beautifully wrapped gift, I had no idea why there was a special twinkle in my mother's eye. We all had a huge laugh as we passed the giant panties around and tried them on. Mother was a large woman, but she, too, modeled the panties. I snuck out of the room to get her camera and catch her in the act.

After Christmas, the *calzones* went into Mother's gift box, a large cardboard bin stored in the living-room closet behind the winter coats and umbrellas. If a birthday came around without warning, if there was an unexpected wedding or a forgotten anniversary, she would send us to the box to find an appropriate last-minute gift. The box held the leftovers given to my mother by her third-grade students, expendable gifts like cheap leather wallets, lifesaver books, inexpensive vases, an assortment of gloves, scarves—and one special item, a red plastic wallet with a window on the front displaying a postcard-size portrait of a handsome and lean Jesus Christ.

We called it the "Jesus wallet," and like the big *calzones*, it was given to one or another family member every Christmas. But unlike the giant panties, the Jesus wallet was a serious gift—too serious for teenage girls. We never used the wallet, but each year, secretly, put it back in the gift box for someone else. By the time another Christmas came around, Mother often forgot which of us had been given the Jesus wallet the year before.

These perennial Christmas gifts were but two of the many presents we received each year from our mother. She never gave us each one or two, or even six or eight gifts. The numbers ranged into the twenties and sometimes thirties. Christmas with my mother never meant lack but overabundance. She gave and gave and then gave more. She was the most generous person I have ever known. If she gave you two or three pairs of socks, they were never wrapped together. Each pair had its own distinctive paper, bow, and gift tag. If she gave you a pair of shoes, each one was wrapped separately.

You could count on a huge individual pile of gifts. One by one, each daughter opened her gifts, and then ceremoniously tried on her clothing, hats and shoes, displayed and commented on any number of offbeat and original items. The process took a long time, but time was all we had then. To our mother's delight, after we'd tried on every single outfit, we'd leave them on display in the living room for several days, draped over the couch. Later, when I became the caretaker of my elderly father, I found myself doing the same thing. I laid out all his gifts on the couch for him to see, his new outfits, his new towels and blankets, his flannel pajamas, his Velcro tennis shoes.

Mother was so proud to see us wearing the things she'd given us. She was an impeccable seamstress and made many of our dresses and suits, purses, pillows, blankets and quilts. Anything you wanted or needed, she could copy. We complained as we stood on wooden chairs in the TV room while she pinned up our skirts or marked a chalk line on the spot where a hem should go. I often whined while she ordered me to "Turn, turn, no, too far, go back." But I loved the clothes she made us. And we loved her, although she sometimes scared us.

Mother could be more imposing than Sister Alma Sophie, the principal at Holy Cross Elementary School, known for her strictness and the lingering smell of her false teeth. Mother could be tougher than Father Ryan, known for his intractable one-sided stance, his Hollywood good looks, wasted on a priest. My mother was the original bogeywoman, a disciplinarian who stopped us with her upraised hand and a razor sharp "*Ya*, that's enough." A "*Ya*" from her could stop a speeding train.

My parents split up when I was ten. The divorce dealt a great blow to my mother's spirit, but it didn't prevent her from inviting my father to spend Christmas and many other holidays with us, nor did it prevent him from accepting her many invitations. Whenever he drove down to Las Cruces from his home in Santa Fe, he always remembered to bring along his dirty laundry, thrown carelessly into the trunk and onto the back seat of his old pea-green Pontiac. A banged-up mess of a car, Mother nicknamed it "Jaws" for its gaping trunk held down by several twisted coat hangers. Daddy never stayed too long or brought too many clean clothes. Each year, religiously, he would make the long trek from his northern home to southern New Mexico to be with his family for Christmas. He always arrived late, sometimes slightly tipsy, other times fully drunk. And he always left much too soon. At first, he shared my mother's bedroom. After a few years, he began to sleep in the TV room, although I can't say with certainty that he didn't cross her threshold once or twice. They loved each other passionately but had little in common. My mother was a devout Catholic who went to church at six o'clock every morning. My father was an alcoholic who loved people, especially women. He liked to stay out late, and to him, freedom meant everything.

Mother was probably even more generous with my father than she was with us, and his pile of gifts was always high. Daddy was never much of a shopper. He bought his clothing at Kmart and his presents at Bonanza City. Daddy bought everything at the last minute. There were years he didn't buy anything at all—not even a gift for his aged mother, who doted on him and was always waiting for his visits. He might give Mother a toaster, a set of steak knives, or a telephone notepad, his wonderful rolling handwriting on the back: "To Mother with Love, Daddy."

One year he bought my sister and me flouncy, frilly dresses that were much too babyish for the grown-up young ladies we had become. I was deeply embarrassed by this thoughtlessness, mortified to be given such a silly thing. The dress fit me and I wore it on Christmas Day, but I hated being seen in such a "little girl's" outfit. To my father, we were still his babies. He knew so little about us. His stories and memories were stale and outdated.

Once he gave us money to buy our mother a gift, and took us to a discount store where we bought all sorts of useless and inexpensive things. I felt badly that we had to buy her such junk and even worse that my father was so cheap. Mother just blinked at her ugly gifts.

A few years before she died, when I had a little money, I gave her a mother-of-pearl ring. It was the only really good gift I ever gave my mother. The ring came in a little box and she gasped with joy when she opened it. I remembered the adage "Big gifts come in small boxes."

It never mattered to my mother what gifts she received, or so she said. What mattered was the gifts she gave to us.

WHEN I THINK of my life, it's times like Christmas I miss the most. Before midnight mass, friends and relatives might drop by our house for my mother's famous tacos, her high, light *sopaipillas*, her *frijoles*, chile and *arroz* or her *pan*, which she made with tortilla dough. Not much of a cook year-round, Mother came to life at Christmas. My sister and I roamed through the house, replenishing food and picking up dirty plates. I yelled from the dining room, to everyone's delight, "*¡Delfina, más tacos!*"

I savor my memories of those Christmas Eve masses in that long ago when St. Genevieve's Church was still standing proud. I tried so hard to stay awake during the interminable rotations of kneeling, standing, and sitting, the Communion walk a needed respite from inertia. My father stood in the back with all the other men, while we women took any available seat we could find. (My mother swore she could tell my father's cough from anyone else's in the crowd.) As we lumbered out of the church around one-thirty Christmas morning, my father would join us. The cold, brisk December air hit us, but not too harshly, for our winters were always mild and it rarely snowed.

We rode home through an immense darkness, eagerly anticipating the opening of gifts. We usually went to bed at two or three a.m., that delicious time when sleep comes gently and so easily. We'd sleep late the next morning, knowing we'd already fulfilled our religious obligations by going to mass the night before. Those early morning hours were so sweet, so magical. They were a time of no time, a time that fulfilled and satisfied and brought peace and love. We lay in bed full of tacos and *capirotada*, my mother's wonderful bread pudding, her *empanadas de calabacita*, and the family mincemeat dish we called "pasta," made exclusively by the Chávez women. It was handed down from Grandma Lupe and kept alive by my aunt Elsie, whose recipe stated that the pasta needed to be cooked "until it looks like caca."

On Christmas Day we'd go to my uncle Sammie's house on the next block, for his famous *menudo*, then drop in on my aunt Elsie Chilton, who lived at the end of our short street. My father's younger sister, Aunt Elsie, was the unofficial Chávez family matriarch and the caregiver for over thirty years of my father's mother, Grandma Lupe. A wizened lady of advanced age with a powdered pale face, she looked a lot like George Washington. Grandma Lupe lived to the left side of Aunt Elsie's laundry room, and it was her duty to fold the clothing for my aunt's eight children. A set of wooden shelves held all of my grandmother's worldly possessions: statues of Our Lady of Guadalupe and St. Jude, myriad rosaries, boxes of greeting cards, soft handkerchiefs (each of them folded and refolded countless times), old Christmas wrap, and faded photographs of her children both living and dead.

My aunt's Christmas trees were always long, thin afterthoughts, never much to look at. My grandmother sat in her wheelchair in her usual spot in the center of the room, peering out like a bird and then calling out with joy as she saw her favorite son, "Chano!"

Aunt Elsie's family was large and boisterous. The children and parents chose names each year and bought a gift only for the person whose name they had selected. My mother always brought gifts for my grandmother, my aunt and uncle, and for her goddaughter, Charlotte, whom my grandmother, in her soft *Mejicano* accent, sounding out the long "ch," called "Charlie."

Mother stocked up on Christmas gifts all year long, and she was likely to have a gift for everyone, she delighted so in giving gifts to those she loved. Not enough gifts came her way, ever. Born on December 24, she said she got cheated at Christmas. But it didn't matter. She loved to give us her extra boxes of Life Savers, along with the usual gifts of socks, panties, nightgowns, bathrobes, stationery, posters, stuffed toys, hair ornaments—and all sorts of unusual items that came our way from her many charities, like the handmade holy cards made by the reclusive Mexican nuns of the Good Shepherd, or the roll of toilet paper genteelly covered by a doll she'd bought at the senior citizen's gift shop.

WHEN I GREW OLDER and moved away, Mother always had large bags of toilet paper for me and for my father as well. Before I drove off after a visit she'd give me her benediction, crossing my forehead with her thumb, as she hugged me hard, her eyes full of tears.

I wonder whatever happened to the Jesus wallet. I'd love to see it again. And who forgot to pass along the big *calzones?* What errant soul failed to keep the legacy alive, the tradition going strong?

I saw my mother die too young of liver cancer and then watched the slow, inexorable passage of my brilliant but troubled father into dementia from Alzheimer's disease.

CHRISTMAS WILL ALWAYS be special to me, as much for its wonderful noisy fanfare as for its deep and pensive silence. After all was said and done, our little street, La Colonia, was asleep but for the one house with its trinity of windows, a blue- or pink- or white- or silver-flocked tree in the corner of the living room, lights woven through the branches covered in angel hair. The incredible pile of presents underneath was so high it scattered halfway across the room. Nearby tables and surfaces held the spillover.

Contented, we dragged ourselves to bed, our family at peace, our disappointments, petty disagreements, and arguments tabled for another day. The cousins and the uncles and aunts were long asleep. My sister and I were tucked in, our father safe at home at least for a little while. Mother, her long black hair flowing down her back, her full bosom heaving happily, turned off all but the Christmas-tree lights. She stood in the doorway to her room, her face moist, a little red dot of color on each cheek. Her door was left open a crack, and would stay that way as she waited for that one special late-night visitor.

The Jesus wallet lay on the coffee table in the living room, ready to be tucked into a dark corner of the gift box. The big *calzones* were draped over the couch like a banner.

The night was beautiful, silent, still. There was no jarring whistle from the train at the end of the block, that train that moved forever north to Albuquerque and then Santa Fe.

In the clear and dark morning, that blessed early morning, the calm was broken only by the sound of muffled voices, rustling bodies, hope.

New Mexican Sopaipillas

FRIED BREAD PILLOWS

These "little pillows" are popular throughout Arizona and New Mexico, where they are served hot in a bread basket, to be dipped in honey, sprinkled with cinnamon sugar, or split open and filled with beans or cheese. Many people are loath to fry things in lard these days (although it has less saturated fat than butter) and it's fine to substitute a solid vegetable shortening. Don't try to fry them up in a liquid oil, though. They just won't puff properly.

2 cups flour	¾ cup warm water or milk
2 teaspoons baking powder	solid vegetable shortening or lard for
1 teaspoon salt	deep frying
2 tablespoons lard or butter	honey, cinnamon sugar

The dough

Sift together the flour, baking powder, and salt. Work in the butter or lard, crumbling it into the dry ingredients a little at a time and working it through thoroughly with your fingers or a pastry cutter. You shouldn't be able to see any bits of shortening. Add the warm water or milk a little at a time, stirring quickly with a fork until it is all worked in. The dough should be pliable and just slightly sticky. If all the dry ingredients aren't absorbed, add a little more liquid, a few drops at a time until the dough is smooth. Knead gently on a lightly floured board, folding it over and punching it down several times. Cover the bowl with a towel and allow the dough to rest at least 30 minutes.

The *sopaipillas* will puff up better if you have time to let the dough rest longer—2 to 3 hours is ideal.

Shaping and frying

Traditionally, *sopaipillas* are shaped like little triangles. Divide the dough in half and roll each half between your hands to make a fat sausage. Roll each piece out to make a rectangular shape about 3 inches wide and quite thin, only about $\frac{1}{8}$ to $\frac{1}{4}$ inch thick. Using a knife, cut triangles end to end from the rectangle. Each triangle should be about the size of a small biscuit.

Cover a tray or platter with a double layer of brown paper or paper towels and have it ready next to the stove. In a heavy skillet, heat shortening about $1\frac{1}{2}$ inches deep until it is hot but not smoking. The temperature of the oil is critical to properly puffed and browned *sopaipillas*. When a few drops of water sprinkled on the surface bubble and pop immediately, the oil is hot enough. If it starts to smoke, turn down the heat and wait for the oil to cool off a little before you proceed.

Drop a dough triangle into the hot oil and immediately hold it under the oil with a slotted spoon, or keep spooning oil on top. In a few seconds the triangle should puff up like a little balloon. Turn it over and fry for a few seconds on the other side. The puff should be a light golden color. Once you have the technique down, you'll be able to fry two or three puffs at a time.

Remove the puffs from the oil immediately and allow to drain. Serve piping hot with honey or cinnamon sugar on the side.

Makes about 25 sopaipillas

Jaime Manrique

*Jaime Manrique was born and raised in Colombia. He is the author of the
novels* Colombian Gold *(Clarkson Potter),* Latin Moon in Manhattan
(St. Martin's Press) and Twilight at the Equator *(Faber and Faber). His most
recent works are* My Night with Federico García Lorca *(Painted Leaf Press),
a collection of poetry, and* Sor Juana's Love Poems *(co-translated with Joan
Larkin). Forthcoming in 1999 is his autobiography,* Eminent Maricones. *He
has been a teacher in the MFA Program at Columbia University, and at the
New School for Social Research and Mount Holyoke College.*

MERRY CRISIS AND A
HYPER NEW YEAR!

I GREW UP in Barranquilla, on the Atlantic Coast of Colombia.
Normally a steamy cauldron, this Caribbean port is cooled each
December by trade winds that bring crisp evenings and intima-
tions of the Christmas season. Springlike conditions prevail, the *lluvia de oro*
trees and the *matarratones* blooming golden and lavender, looking like Christmas trees hung with neon lights.

The first pre-Christmas event in Colombia is La Noche de las Velitas on
December 7. Celebrants decorate their front porches with hundreds of candles and colored lanterns. The families who observe this tradition stay up all

night partying. At dawn, the revelers join the procession of the Virgin of the Immaculate Conception, whose feast day this is.

The next three weeks are like an ongoing Fourth of July: The nights become resplendent with the voices of children burning sparklers (which we know in Colombia by the more poetic name of "Bengal Lights") and with the overlapping noises of the *triquitraques*. Makeshift wooden *castillos* are built, and when they are set alight, crowds gather to admire brilliant displays of pyrotechnics.

Every year, my family journeyed to El Banco, a town on the shores of the Magdalena River, to spend Navidades at my grandparents' house. There, the Ardilas clan (my mother's people) assembled: my grandparents, their twelve children, and all the grandchildren. We arrived by Christmas Eve and stayed until New Year's Day.

I can remember congregating at night in the town's main church to sing *villancicos*, our carols. Of course, we exchanged *aguinaldos*, and on Christmas morning there were the gifts *el niño Dios* had brought. But not all my memories of Christmas in Colombia are so happy.

Recently, I called my sister to probe her memory about our childhood Navidades. "All I remember," she snorted, "was the men pulling out their rifles and guns and firing them into the sky, scaring me to death!" Yes, I also remembered this terrifying display of machismo.

My sister got me thinking. What else did I remember about these family gatherings? Then, slowly, it all came back to me: the real excitement of the holidays was provided by the seasonal family crises. Every year it was the turn of another of my young aunts to announce a romance. It seemed that—no matter who the suitor—my grandfather would automatically find him unworthy.

Christmas was not complete without one of the lovelorn *tías* trying to commit suicide by swallowing boxes of matches or dozens of firecrackers, or by slashing her wrists. When my aunts really wanted to scare us, they announced they were going to take rat poison. Fortunately, none of them ever went that far.

So while the aromas of *ayacas*, coconut rice, *arroz con leche*, and *natillas* emanated from the kitchen, life-and-death melodramas took place in the women's quarters. As stuffed turkeys and cinnamon-scented *enyucados* came out of the oven, and rice *pasteles* were wrapped in plantain leaves, the older women darted hysterically from the kitchen to the bedrooms of my aunts to save a life or two. It was a strain on the married women to make sure that the *pernil de puerco* was done to perfection, just before accompanying a younger woman to the hospital, or to remember to mix all the ingredients in the *pasteles* before they met with the doctors who constantly came by the house.

My young uncles, too, fell in love. They dramatized their plights by getting drunk and smashing the Jeep against a huge termite mound. We took love seriously in our family.

The annual holiday season closed on New Year's Day at my grandfather's farm, where there was usually at least one female nursing a bandaged wrist, another lying in a hammock, too weak to walk as a result of having had her stomach pumped. There was usually also a young uncle on crutches, wearing a cast and looking as angry as Paul Newman in *Cat on a Hot Tin Roof*. We ate an epic *sancocho*, wondering whose turn it would be the following Christmas. It's no wonder that to this day I dread the mention of Christmas. I was well into my adulthood when I discovered that not all families celebrated the holidays the way mine had. And yet, glutton that I am, I would gladly revisit the past just to eat one of the immortal *pasteles* my aunt Emilia prepared for Nochebuena.

Pasteles de Arroz y de Gallina

RICE AND CHICKEN STEAMED IN PLANTAIN LEAVES

Making *pasteles* can be a community endeavor, like a quilting bee. As part of the holiday celebration, a group of women will get together to chop and prepare the ingredients. Then, sitting around the kitchen table, they wrap the *pasteles* like an assembly line, with one woman preparing the leaves, another stuffing them, a third wrapping, and a fourth tying the packets. The *pasteles* can be made weeks in advance and frozen to be cooked later. This recipe was contributed by Jaime Manrique's "aunt-in-law," Jocabeth de Ardilo.

THE WRAPPERS

30 to 40 prepared plantain leaves, or cooking parchment and aluminum foil

Plantain leaves can be purchased either prepared or raw in markets where tropical produce is sold. To prepare raw leaves: Clean each leaf with a damp cloth. Using shears, cut each into 9- or 10-inch squares. Hold each leaf by the edges, with a pot holder or tongs, over a burner, turning constantly until the leaf begins to change color. Stack leaves and wrap in foil to keep warm. Leaves will get stiff and hard to work with as they cool.

The leaves impart a wonderful flavor to the stuffing inside the packets, but if you can't find them, you can substitute paper and foil. Cut cooking parchment into 6- to 8-inch squares. Then cut 8- to 10-inch squares of foil. For every plantain leaf, use a square of cooking parchment on a square of foil. Wrap so that the foil is on the outside. These little packets have to stand up to a long simmering process.

THE ACHIOTE

1 cup cooking oil *2 tablespoons annatto seeds*

In a cast-iron or heavy skillet, heat ½ cup olive or vegetable oil. When very hot, add annatto seeds. Turn heat to low, continue cooking, stirring frequently, for approximately 5 minutes, until oil is a rich orange-red color. Allow to cool, then strain into a clean glass container. Set aside.

THE RICE

4 pounds rice *4 teaspoons ground cumin*
1 cup achiote *2 teaspoons ground black pepper*
10 to 12 garlic cloves, mashed *salt to taste*
4 large onions, chopped very fine

Wash the rice, drain well. In a big, heavy pot, heat the achiote oil until hot but not smoking. Add the garlic, chopped onions, and the rice. Cook, stirring constantly, until the rice becomes translucent. Add cumin, black pepper, and salt. Stir, then set aside.

THE STUFFING

Olive or vegetable oil for sautéing *1 cup white wine*
1½ pounds pork, cut in small pieces *3 tablespoons tomato paste*
2 green bell peppers, chopped into *2 carrots, chopped fine*
small pieces *2 potatoes, cubed*
1 bunch scallions, sliced fine *1 4-ounce jar green olives, strained and*
5 garlic cloves, chopped fine *chopped*
3 to 4 pounds chicken, boned and cut *1 4-ounce jar capers*
into small pieces
1 tablespoon powdered adobo
(a spice mixture available in the
interna-tional section of many
supermarkets)

Oil the bottom of a heavy skillet, and sauté the pork for 5 minutes, stirring constantly so the meat cooks evenly. Then add the peppers, scallions, and garlic, cook for 2 minutes more, then add the chicken. Stir until the chicken begins to turn white, then add the other ingredients. Cook for about 10 to 15 minutes more. Vegetables will not be cooked completely at this point.

THE PASTELES

plantain leaves
½ cup olive oil in a bowl
rice mixture

stuffing mixture
enough salted water to cover

Lay a warm prepared plantain leaf flat on the table. Using a pastry brush, brush the center of one side lightly with olive oil. Place 2 heaping tablespoons of rice mixture in the center of the leaf. Top with 1 heaping tablespoon of stuffing mixture. Fold two long edges over the filling, then fold the open ends toward the center. Don't wrap too tightly, because the rice is going to expand. Cut about 1 yard of kitchen string and fold in half. Place folded string on the table with the loop facing you. Place the seam side of 2 *pasteles* together. Put the 2 *pasteles* in the middle of the string. Pull the ends of the string around the *pasteles* and through the loop. Pull the loose ends until the loop is in the middle of the *pastel.* Pull the two string ends in opposite directions towards the narrow ends of the *pasteles.* Turn *pasteles* over and tie the strings together in the middle.

Arrange *pasteles* on the bottom of large pot. *Pasteles* can be stacked three or four layers deep. Cover with salted water and bring to a boil. Lower heat and continue to simmer. After about 90 minutes, unwrap one of the *pasteles* and check for doneness. Serve in the packets. To eat, cut the twine, slide the stuffing out of the leaves, and enjoy!

Makes 30 to 40 pasteles

EN BRAZOS DE UNA DONCELLA

A Christmas Song from Ecuador

En brazos de una doncella, un
    infante se dormía.
En brazos de una doncella, un
    infante de dormía.

Y decirte lo que siento en mi pobre
    corazón,
Quisiera niñito adorado, calentarte
    con mi aliento,
Y decirte lo que siento, en mi pobre
    corazón.

Upon the arms of a virgin, an infant
    slept.
Upon the arms of a virgin, an infant
    slept.

I would like to tell you what I feel in
    my poor heart,
Adored Child, to warm you with my
    breath,
And to tell you what is in my heart.

Michael Nava

Michael Nava grew up in Sacramento, California. He is the author of the Henry Ríos mysteries, a detective series featuring a gay Chicano criminal defense lawyer. His most recent book is The Burning Plain *(Putnam).*

CHARITY

I WAS RAISED on welfare. This was not so unusual in Gardenland, the Sacramento neighborhood where I grew up. It had always been a place where poor people lived. Most of us descended either from Mexican immigrants or Dustbowl Okies. My maternal family had lived there since the 1920s. My grandmother's family had been driven out of Mexico by the civil war that followed the Revolution of 1910. My grandfather was a Yaqui Indian, and his family had fled from Mexico to Arizona at the turn of the century to escape the invasion of their homeland in the Sonoran Desert by the federal army of Porfirio Díaz. In Gardenland, they managed to achieve a modest, working-class affluence. My mother, however, their eldest daughter, did not fare as well.

Christmas was celebrated at my grandparents' house on Christmas Day, American-style, with a tree and a turkey dinner. Only my grandmother retained any connection to Mexican traditions and the only vestige of them were the tamales she served alongside the turkey. Among the piles of presents beneath the tree, there were always a few for my brothers and sisters and me, but these came from my grandparents or my aunts and uncles. My mother,

scraping by on AFDC checks, could not afford presents, even for her own children, much less her nephews and nieces, which made Christmas a difficult time for her.

Then one year our family was chosen by the local chapter of the Lions' Club as one of the poor families whom the Club would sponsor at Christmas. This not only meant a basket of food would be delivered to our house on Christmas Eve, complete with our very own turkey, but also that we kids would be taken to a party at the Lions' clubhouse where Santa Claus would give each of us a present.

One of my aunts once told me that as a teenager my mother had been "as pretty as Rita Hayworth," but by the time she was in her midthirties, with six kids and a husband in jail, her face had become a puddle of indistinct features held together by worry. But I was a kid and, except for the nickels I needed for candy and comic books, money meant nothing to me. Moreover, it was different being poor in the fifties and sixties than it is today, at least in Gardenland. Drugs and gangs had not yet entered the picture, nor were the poor despised as they are now, because poverty was still considered a circumstance that could be improved rather than a moral failing that could not. And Gardenland, as its name suggests, was a rural neighborhood where people grew some of their own food in vegetable gardens and old women, like my grandmother, kept flocks of chickens for eggs and meat. Moreover—and this is the most important thing—Gardenland was an isolated community, not so much on the wrong side of the tracks as a place the tracks never reached. We all lived the same way. There was nothing to which I could have compared us, that would have shown me how poor we were.

My mother, however, knew to the last penny how bad things were. She was the one who had to beg for extensions to pay the rent and for credit at the corner store. Poverty also forced her to forgo her pride and deliver her children to strangers who could give them things she could not, because this is a choice the poor must often face—to keep their children in certain destitution or to give them away to the possibility of a better life. It was clear from an early age that I was a child fated to be given away. I was a curious, precocious boy who buried his head in books and looked far beyond the shantytown horizons of Gardenland. Throughout my childhood my mother gradually surrendered me to the world of white people, and it was there that I discovered how badly off we really were.

The Lions held their Christmas party in an auditorium in downtown Sacramento. I remember a big, brightly lit room furnished for the occasion with tables covered by red-and-green tablecloths, each with a centerpiece of gilded pinecones, holly, and candles. A long table at the back of the room held bowls of punch and plates of sweets. There were a couple of hundred children, most of us black or brown. We all wore our best clothes, enjoined not to get them dirty. There were always tears when someone scuffed her new shoes or spilled punch on his white shirt. We loaded paper plates with cookies, candies, and cake, and carried them, along with plastic glasses of punch, to our sponsor's table. The front of the room served as a stage from which we were entertained by a magician or a church choir singing the traditional carols, but they were merely a prelude. Behind them was an immense Christmas tree, its pine scent filling the room. Ropes of colored light twined through the dark branches hung with globes and tinsel. At the very top, almost scraping the ceiling, was a gold star bordered in tiny white lights. Beneath the tree were piles of presents gorgeously wrapped in silver and gold, red and green, and tied with bright ribbons and lavish bows. Next to them was a thronelike chair from which Santa Claus dispensed the bounty.

For most of us kids, the heaps of presents represented such unimaginable plenty that at first it hardly mattered what was inside them. But as the afternoon wore on and we filled ourselves with sugar, astonishment gave way to excitement, excitement to impatience, and impatience to anxiety that maybe there wouldn't be enough presents to go around. By the time Santa Claus emerged from the wings on a sleigh pushed by green-clad helper elves, the mood in the hall was not so much joy as agitation. It failed to occur to the good-hearted Lions, as they planned the party's little treats and surprises, that instead of delighting the poor children of Sacramento, the magician and the choir would only prolong our anxiety about the presents. We were kids who didn't have anything and to have these riches dangled in front of us was enough, really, to make us all a little crazy.

After a brief speech about how he had checked his list of good children and found our names on it, Santa distributed the presents with the help of an elf who handed him the packages from beneath the tree. After Santa read the name of the child for whom the gift was intended, he or she walked to the front of the room to accept it while a photographer memorialized the moment. With a couple of hundred kids, the ceremony took time and well before it was over any remaining gaiety had been replaced by restlessness. We were admonished not to open our presents until we got home, but some kids couldn't wait, and ripped through the shiny wrapping paper even as they walked back to their tables. Inevitably, they were disappointed because the present was not selected for the particular child but generically—dolls for girls, Lincoln Logs for boys, that kind of thing. At the end, the party felt no different to me than waiting in the hallway of the county hospital to have my eyes or teeth checked. But when I came home, and my mother asked me if I'd had a good time, I knew enough to tell her yes.

I was ten years old the last time I went to a Lions' Club Christmas party. By then I understood this was not a real party to which I had been invited because the hosts either knew or liked me. I had been asked only because we were poor, and I understood that one of the jobs of poor people is to be the object of charity. For whatever reason, out of some precocious sense of dignity or mere ingratitude, I did not wish to be one of the needy children on behalf of whom the Lions appealed to the public for toys. It was one thing to accept gifts from aunts and uncles who were better off than we were, because they were family and family provided for each other and there was no shame in it. Accepting charity from strangers was to be held up and labeled not just poor—but inferior.

In a rare act of rebellion, I refused to go, but by then two of my siblings were old enough to be included, and my mother appealed to the good boy in me to take care of them. Mingled in that appeal was another, unspoken, plea: that I not judge her harshly for what she had to do to give something to her children they would not otherwise have. In that moment she made herself my equal, and I could not refuse her.

Our sponsor arrived. The three of us piled into his car, where a couple of other kids were already waiting, and we went off to the party. As soon as we entered the hall, I saw the tree and the presents and thought about having to make the march from our table to the front of the room to accept my generic gift. My stomach began to churn. Still obedient to my mother, I took my little brother and sister in hand and showed them the tree, the presents, and Santa's throne, and let them fill their little bellies with sweets. But their excitement only made me feel guilty, because I knew I had initiated them into something that was not quite what it seemed.

I sat worriedly through the afternoon, scarcely eating or drinking, waiting for the moment when my name would be called. At last, I heard Santa say, "Mike Nava."

I slouched down in my seat.

"That's you," my sponsor said.

"Mike Nava?" Santa repeated.

I looked down at my plate of half-eaten cake, refusing to meet my sponsor's eyes as he said, "Mike, go get your present."

"No," I whispered.

"Mike Nava?" Santa said, a little impatiently this time. "Where's Mike?"

The metal legs of my sponsor's chair squeaked against the linoleum as he stood up and strode decisively to the front of the room where he accepted my present from Santa, who joked that "Mike" seemed pretty big for his age.

"Here," my sponsor said, handing me the gift. "What's wrong with you? Do you feel okay?"

"My stomach hurts," I mumbled.

"Oh, why didn't you say so," he replied. "You have to use the bathroom? The toilet?"

I nodded.

"You know where it is?"

"Yes," I said.

I got up and made my way among the tables of clamoring kids to the bathroom, where I sat on the toilet, even though I didn't really have to go, until I thought enough time had passed for me to return to the party. I washed my hands at the sink, in case my sponsor checked, and stared at my face in the mirror. I was crying. I washed my face and went back for the rest of the party. When my sponsor dropped me off at home and my mother asked me if I'd had a good time, I tossed my unwrapped present aside and said, "Next time, I'm not going."

She studied my face, looked sad, and replied, "I'm sorry you didn't have a good time, *m'hijo*. The kids will be old enough to go by themselves next year."

The next day I scratched out my name on the tag of my still-unopened Lions' Club present and asked my mother if we could stop at the fire station on the way to my grandparents' house. I knew the firemen also collected presents for poor families. She pulled up and I ran in and shoved the gift into the hand of the first grown-up I saw

Holiday Punch

No kid grows up in the United States without being subjected to some sort of fruit punch, with or without the help of the local Lions' Club. The punch bowl can be filled with any combination of juice and soda. In Mexico, the *Ponche de Navidad* often includes indigenous fruits, like guava and *tejocote*, scented with a dash of cinnamon; and for the adults a little tequila, rum, or *vino tinto*. This recipe (typical of the punch served by Lions' Clubs across the country) comes to us courtesy of Marion Cooper of Simi Valley, California. It's easy to make, delicious, and perfect for Christmas parties.

1 12-ounce can each of frozen orange juice and frozen lemonade, diluted

1 48-ounce can of apricot nectar

1 48-ounce can of pineapple juice

1 32-ounce bottle of lemon-lime soda

Mix all ingredients and pour over ice.

Makes 20 servings

$\mathcal{J}$ulia $\mathcal{A}$lvarez

Julia Alvarez is originally from the Dominican Republic, but she immigrated to this country with her parents at the age of ten. She is the author of three novels, How the García Girls Lost Their Accents, In the Time of the Butterflies, *and* ¡Yo!, *two books of poems,* Homecoming *and* The Other Side, *and a forthcoming collection of essays,* Something to Declare. *She teaches at Middlebury College. This story is a fictionalized account of her own experiences growing up in the Trujillo regime in the Dominican Republic.*

SWITCHING TO SANTICLÓ

"HE'S GOING TO COME through the roof?" I asked. I didn't like the sound of it.

My cousin Fico, who was usually my informer in the ways of the world, was telling me how Santicló would deliver his gifts in a few days. Ever since the Americans had occupied the country and put our dictator in place, customs from up north had replaced the old ways. Now we would be getting presents from big, fat, blue-eyed Santicló. That is, if either of us were getting any gifts. As the two hellions in the family, we had already been told that Santicló would probably just bring us cat poopoo in a shoe box.

I liked it much more when *niño* Jesus brought us presents. Even if we only got one present apiece, it was guaranteed. He reserved hell for people who didn't behave, but He didn't spoil Christmas by bringing up punishments.

That was not His way.

He also didn't come down through the roof in the middle of the night and scare you half to death. Christmas morning beside the crèche under the sea-grape tree painted white and blooming out of a paint can covered in tinfoil, you found your bicycle with the long plastic ribbons coming out of the handles, or hanging from one of the sea-grape branches was your cowgirl outfit. If only it had been a cowboy outfit with a holster like Fico's instead of a sissy pocketbook with a vanity mirror! But to say so was to be ungrateful to *el niño* Jesus, which wasn't a nice thing to do to a baby who was going to grow up and be crucified. In this way, Santicló might be better. He might listen to complaints. He might take returns.

"He might be here late, though, because he's got to come down from Nueva York," Fico went on, a grin spreading on his face.

That did sound promising. Nueva York was where toys came from. Whenever our grandparents went north, they came back with suitcases full of games and puzzles and paddle balls and plastic sheets you could draw on, lift the sheets, and—abracadabra—the drawing was gone! And, of course, practical things like school shoes and book bags and Russell Stover chocolates that you studied carefully when the box went by to be sure you picked one that didn't have something yucky inside. Ever so gently you pressed with the ball of your finger to see if it was a taker—one with nuts or with more chocolate in the center. Quickly, you popped it into your mouth, and then, if you were Fico or me, you opened your mouth in midchew to show off your prize to the prim girl cousins. "Mami," they wailed in chorus, "they're being bad again."

"I'm asking for a trampoline and a little airplane that flies and a *carrito* I can drive myself!" Fico was yelling as if he wanted Santicló to hear him all the way up in the United States. Each new present was pronounced at a higher decibel than the one before it.

I was sick with envy. My cousin always had so many toys. His parents were rich and traveled to Miami and Nueva York and took him along. But Mami had married Papi who didn't have that kind of money. In fact, Papi's family lived in the interior in houses with crooked floors and furniture like the rockers in the maid's room at my maternal grandparents' house. Papi's brothers were always in trouble with the dictator. One uncle, Tío Federico, was a lawyer who had to stay in the house all the time because he had done something he shouldn't have done. Another, Tío Puchulo, had written something in the papers that made all the aunts walk around with their hands at their hearts and their eyes as big as the eyes of people in movies when they got a fright.

I decided to holler out my list as well. Maybe Santicló would listen and bring me everything I asked for. "I want a trampoline and a flying airplane and a television."

"I'm asking for a television, too," Fico piped up.

"I asked first!"

"You did not!"

We were almost touching chins, yelling at each other. I could feel my cousin's moist breath on my face. Soon we would be rolling around on the ground, punching each other, until one of the maids came out and separated us and took us to our mothers, who would remind us that Santicló was coming next week and all he was going to bring us was two boxes of cat poopoo.

That thought made me stop midholler. "Fico," I relented, "maybe we'd better stop. Maybe Santicló can hear us."

Fico shrugged. "Santicló speaks English, stupid. He doesn't understand us." But he stopped yelling, too, just in case Santicló was like Tío Puchulo, who always said that just because he didn't know any English didn't mean he didn't understand it.

SPEAKING OF Tío Puchulo, where was he? Just a few days ago, he was the name on everyone's lips on account of something he wrote in the papers. Then, like those sheets from the United States you drew on and lifted, abracadabra, he disappeared. "Where's Tío Puchulo?" I asked a few days before Christmas when he didn't appear for Sunday dinner. The whole patio of aunts and uncles and my grandparents went silent. My mother gave me that look the girl cousins gave me when I showed them my Russell Stover prize midchew.

"Why do you ask where your *tío* Puchulo is?" she asked me too lightly to sound like my mother talking.

This was the stupidest question I'd ever heard. "Because he's not here."

"Oh," everyone sighed and laughed with apparent relief. "Of course he's not here. Your *tío* left the capital."

"We don't know where he is," my mother added quickly. One of the maids had just come out to the patio with the rolling cart of platters.

"Let's talk about Santicló, shall we?" one of the aunts asked cheerfully. There was a raucous YES! from the kids' table. "What does everyone want for Christmas?" Soon we were hollering our lists so loud, my aunt put a finger in each ear and rolled her eyes like a crazy person.

When dinner was over, my mother pulled me aside. "Cuca," she said, her lovey-dovey name for me when she wanted something. "Do you want Santicló to bring you that TV?"

"Santicló's going to bring me a TV?!!!" I cried out.

"Well," Mami hesitated. "Maybe he'll bring one for the whole family."

"Oh." That dampened my happiness. In Fico's house, they had one TV for his parents, one for the kids, and one for the maids. And now he was even asking for one to have in his very own room. But even a shared TV was better than none at all.

"But darling Cuca, Mami thinks you'd better not mention your *tío* Puchulo's name. You see, Santicló doesn't like him. If Santicló hears you mentioning his name, I'm afraid that TV won't make it down here on his sled."

As far as I was concerned, Santicló had very poor taste if he didn't like my uncle. Tío Puchulo was fun. Sundays, when he came over, he'd ask the boy cousins if they wanted to see the angels' panties, and if they said yes, he lifted them by their ankles, so they could look upside down at the sky. And if you got a bad chocolate, girl or boy, Tío Puchulo always called you over and pulled a chiclet out of his pocket. But a TV was a TV. I gave my word I wouldn't mention my uncle's name.

"There's a good girl," my mother said. It was the first time in ages she'd said that about me.

ON CHRISTMAS EVE, my grandparents threw a big party. All the grand-children came for a little while, but before the uncles started tangoing on the dining room table or throwing themselves into the pool, we were marched home. Tonight nobody complained. We knew Santicló would not come until all the children in the world had fallen asleep.

From my bedroom, I could hear the party going in the distance. Iluminada, the old nursemaid, helped us into our babydolls, and then we knelt down in a row to say our prayers. As I was going through my long list of whom I wanted God to take care of—my grandparents, my mother, my father, my aunts, my uncles—Tío Puchulo's name popped out.

I clapped my hand over my mouth. I looked up at Lumi. Maybe she hadn't heard me?

"Why not pray for your *tío* Puchulo?" she said in a fierce, low voice. "May God help him," she added, making the sign of the cross.

"But Santicló doesn't like him," I explained.

"Santicló!" she snapped. "Your parents are bringing you up *sin principios*." Scolds were usually delivered en masse, even if there had only been one offender. "All of you praying to a big fat white man in a red suit like the devil! You ask *niño* Jesus for forgiveness, and maybe He'll come back again to this house and lift the heaviness that is here."

I never listened much to what the grown-ups had to say unless there was a TV involved or a visit to the ice cream shop or a squirt gun or a paddleball. But Lumi always made sense to me. She could read my coffee cup and tell me I was going to go away soon to another country where I would switch languages, homes, schools, friends, hopes, and dreams. She had been in my father's family since the Haitian massacre way back before I was even born. My father's mother, whom I had never met, had hidden the terrified Haitian woman and her little boy under a pile of laundry. When the dictator's men searched the house, they found no one. Lumi was devoted to my father's family, but especially to my *tío* Puchulo who had told the soldier ready to poke the laundry with his drawn bayonet, that if he ruined my grandmother's sheets, he was going to have the devil to pay for them.

I fell asleep with a heavy heart. No presents for me, I was sure of it . . .

In the middle of the night, I woke to the sound of footsteps. Someone was moving above my bedroom. Footsteps on the stairs . . . voices . . . hushings. . . . A little later, a car started up. Did Santicló's sled break down? Did he know how to drive a car?

Years later, on safe ground, having escaped to the United States of America, having switched citizenship and languages and homes and dreams—like Lumi said I would—Papi told me the story of how Tío Puchulo had been hidden in an upstairs closet of our house for two weeks before they had found a way to smuggle him out of the country through the interior and across the Haitian border.

Christmas morning, Mami's face was happier, as if some weight had been lifted from her shoulders. And there it was in the *sala* of our house, a TV. But it turned out, in the weeks to come, that there was nothing to watch. Recently, with trouble from rebels and such, programming had been limited to long reports from the national palace. "Be careful what you ask for!" Lumi scolded when I complained.

But what I remember about that first Christmas we switched to Santicló is not the new TV or the subsequent disappointment of having nothing to watch, but how I woke up in the middle of Christmas night to the sound of footsteps above my head, and my heart filled with happiness. Santicló had come, after all! Mami had been wrong. He did like my uncle.

I was oh-so-tempted to go see the presents piled high by the sea-grape tree in the living room. But I couldn't seem to pull myself out of bed. My body felt heavier and heavier as slowly, sheet after sheet after sheet of darkness descended on me, and I fell asleep.

Liz Balmaseda

Liz Balmaseda, a columnist for the Miami Herald, *was awarded the 1993 Pulitzer Prize for commentary. She was* Newsweek's *Central America bureau chief, based in El Salvador, and a field producer for NBC News based in Honduras. The National Association of Hispanic Journalists awarded her the first prize for print in the Guillermo Martinez-Márquez contest; and she was honored by the National Association of Black Journalists for her commentaries on Haiti.*

NEXT YEAR IN HAVANA

 THERE ALWAYS SEEMED to be that one lucky *lechón*, plumped by nostalgia, marinated by exile politics, and always in the end— that lucky pig—spared by Fidel.

It was the one the old Cubans in Miami perennially vowed to consume in Havana the next Nochebuena.

"*Oye chico, el año que viene el lechoncito lo comemos allá . . .*"

Over there.

This would be a *lechón* slaughtered at dawn, skewered with particular satisfaction, lowered into an earth hole in the back yard—or perhaps into one of those tin contraptions they use in *el exilio*, called "*La Caja China.*" It would be slow-roasted to perfection as morning dissolved into afternoon, the cousin population swelled inside the kitchen, and in a rustle of palms the strains of triumph filtered into the night, serenading the martyred *lechoncito* like a Willy Chirino song.

We all asked Santa for bicycles and Barbies.

Mami and Papi and Abuelo and Abuela asked for Christmas in Cuba.

For as long as I can remember, Nochebuena Miami-style has been a feast of fantasy. We would spray our winter wonderlands upon the sliding glass door in the Florida room—¡*Feliz Navidad!*/snowflake/snowflake/snowman/candy cane—oblivious to the contrast of the scene outside, the palm trees and banana trees and oranges and mangos, the Virgencita de la Caridad shrine, the Slip-n-Slide, and the basketball net.

We celebrated a stream of Nochebuenas in Hialeah, the *viejos* invoking the spirits of long-ago celebrations as their sons and daughters picked apart the Miami Dolphins' starting lineup. Our unwitting stabs at assimilation left us in a bizarre time capsule. Consider the juxtaposition of Celia Cruz, Benny Moré, and Joe Cuba with Dasher, Dancer, Prancer, and Vixen.

My uncle sang rum-soaked tangos. My cousin sang Charles Aznavour songs. I chased her into startling octaves with my guitar. We drank eggnog and nibbled *turrón*. And sometime during the night, as inevitably as Christmas would dawn the next day, somebody in the house cried for those left behind in Puerto Padre, Cuba—those who seemed to exist in another dimension, a sad, gray state of inertia.

On Christmas, we could produce evidence of our Cuban roots at the dinner table and on the dance floor. But no amount of black beans and *yuca con mojo* and cha-cha-chá could summon all of Cuba to West Hialeah, Dade County, Florida. The nostalgia-bound had to settle for the fantasy.

In the meantime, we all thought ourselves to be pretty American. After all, we had the American Christmas routine down. We had accomplished layaway and the mall. We anticipated Santa like everybody else. (Of course we knew he had to make extra stops at Cuban families' homes, considering how many cousins and second cousins and aunts and great-aunts and uncles we had.)

What seemed to make us different from *los americanos* was that extra *lechón*, the one always granted a stay of execution when it became clear Nochebuena, once again, would be in Miami.

Over here.

Yuca al Escabeche

YUCA IN GARLIC SAUCE

Yuca is a root vegetable that grows in the tropics. It can be found in the freezers of many supermarkets that carry tropical produce. Esmeralda's mother, Ramona Santiago, makes this dish the night before she serves it, but she prefers to eat her portion warm, right after it's prepared. It's equally delicious at room temperature.

5 pounds yuca

enough salted water to cover

1 cup extra-virgin olive oil

4 to 5 large garlic cloves, peeled and sliced

3 large onions, sliced thin

2 teaspoons whole black peppercorns

2 bay leaves

1 tablespoon vinegar

1 whole roasted sweet red pepper (fresh or canned), chopped

Boil yuca in salted water to cover for 30 minutes or until it can be pierced with a fork but is not too soft. Drain. Slice into 1 1/2-inch-wide slices. Transfer to heat-proof serving dish.

Heat oil in a cast-iron skillet. Add garlic and cook, stirring, just until golden. Add onions, peppercorns, and bay leaves. When onions begin to turn transparent, add vinegar. Add chopped red pepper and cook until just heated. Do not overcook.

Pour sauce over yuca in the dish. Serve warm or at room temperature.

Makes 8 servings

Estela Herrera

Estela Herrera grew up in Mendoza, Argentina. She has lived in the United States since 1968, working extensively as an educator and a journalist in the Spanish-language media. In 1991, she received the National Association of Hispanic Publications Award for Outstanding Editorial Column. She currently teaches at the University of California, Los Angeles, and is working on her first novel.

NURTURING THE WILD BEAST OF CHRISTMAS

IT WAS MID-NOVEMBER in the little western Argentine town of Luján de Cuyo and the heat was relentless. Summer was fragrant with the sweet smell of melons and peaches, a prelude to the annual bounty of Christmas delicacies. Only one more month and these fruits, together with cherries, early apples, and apricots from the neighboring orchards would mingle happily with imported bananas and pineapples in the colorful concoctions that kept the women of the household busy for days peeling, cutting, cooking, and baking.

The air was full of expectations, of foods to enjoy, of people to see. Father had left early that morning, and when I asked why he hadn't taken me along I was hushed and told I should keep quiet because he was bringing home a surprise. And he certainly did.

We lived at the edge of the town, between the asphalt and the vineyards.

From our house we could see the endless, orderly rows of green vines that turned red and yellow in the fall against the blue backdrop of the mountains. The Andes were always blue and mysteriously dangerous: so many stories of people who found their death at the bottom of an abyss or in the snow of a peak. There were no trees and certainly no vineyards on the harsh, rocky slopes.

Father had gone to the mountains that day to meet one of the few people who were, as Auntie put it, either so desperately daring or so desperately poor as to scrape a living from the tough and scant wild bushes that were all the mountains had to offer. When he came back, late and covered with dust, he was holding in his arms a small, warm, and trembling black creature.

"A baby goat, *nena*. Do you like it?"

I loved it instantly! I hardly slept that night, stirred by the anticipation of all the things I could do with the new member of the household. The following morning, I announced my plan over the breakfast table. I was going to feed it twice a day and take it to the vineyards for a walk. At night I was going to bring it indoors so it wouldn't be afraid of the dark. "None of that nonsense," said Father, particularly bringing it into the house. The baby goat was to be kept in a little shed, improvised with chicken wire in the back patio, and I should not involve myself with it at all.

The rules were soon violated. I fed the goat as often as I could without being seen. In the afternoons, when the house succumbed to the heavy stupor of the siesta and everything stood still for two or three hours, I took it to the vineyards where I pointed it to the tender grasses and clover leaves that grew abundantly from the rich soil. "So much better than the thorny weeds of the mountains, don't you think? You will never have to eat them again. I will never let you go back, my poor *chivito*."

In time, the copious leftovers in the shed led the grown-ups to discover my secret activities, but they didn't get very angry. In fact, they seemed to tolerate it with a bit of amusement. So I felt free to talk about my new friend. I struggled for days to find the perfect name for it and was ecstatic when somebody suggested Azabache. Jet stone. I was very young then and still blessed with a sense of astonishment when confronted with the obvious or the banal. I thought the name was strikingly original and so appropriate.

Azabache was a constant source of pleasure. The way its big eyes looked at me, its clumsy walk on the coarsely tilled soil beyond the asphalt, or the way it jumped and frolicked for no reason at all. I lived with and for Azabache.

By mid-December, Azabache had grown considerably while the adults' amusement with my obsession had sharply dwindled. Christmas preparations had begun full tilt and the house was a harried tumult of skirts coming and going, cleaning, polishing, shopping, planning. The Nativity scene was disinterred and the peeling paint on San José's cloak had to be retouched. The aroma of freshly baked *pan dulce* wafted from the kitchen, redolent with vanilla and candied fruit. Nobody noticed I had stolen some of the sugary lemon and orange rinds. I was so proud of myself that I was taken aback when Azabache met my offering with utter indifference. It refused to even taste them. A few days later, the pineapples and bananas were bought and placed in the warmest corners of the house to ensure their precise ripeness for the *clericó*, the fruit salad of the season, laced with orange juice for children, with champagne or vermouth for adults.

That holiday season my days were divided between the back patio and the vineyards—I hardly visited the kitchen. Azabache was far more fun than the adults who had grown increasingly silent. But the fact that they lowered their voices when I came in or avoided my eyes bothered me only a little, since I had already experienced the whimsical ways of grown-ups, who were always changing the rules for obscure reasons or no reason at all. God only knew why they were acting so peculiar. Was Father angry at them? Just too much to do? After all, Mother and the other women were really very busy frying flaky quince turnovers, plucking chickens, and pressing the stuffed beef rolls for the *matambre*. No time for silly conversations with me. They needed to prepare the bite-size beef *empanadas* and the diminutive *sandwiches de miga*, moist towers of *pain de mie*, ham, red pimentos, cheese, and tender lettuce.

On the night of December 23 I went to bed happy knowing that cousins Irma, Amanda, and María Luisa were coming. We would all take Azabache for a walk, and in the early evening, when the heat had eased, help set the tables in the garden. We would eat many wonderful treats and play until past midnight. We would talk about the gifts we were expecting on January 6 from the Three Wise Kings, while trying to keep count of the fireflies—our favorite summer pastime—shouting over the deafening choir of crickets. Mother and her sisters would blame our loudness, as they always did, on my father's largess in allowing us to drink a little alcoholic apple cider.

I slept soundly only to be awakened by a loud, sharp scream such as I never heard before. It came from the back patio, lacerating the early morning light and stabbing me in the heart. There was nothing in the world but that scream and my pain. And suddenly I knew. I understood the silence of the previous days and the women's feigned indifference toward me. I jumped out of bed and rushed to the front door. I ran out of the house in a frenzy, choked by my own scream stuck in my throat. I ran into the vineyards, stumbling on the moist soil, toward the blue mountains where Azabache had come from and I knew he would never, ever, go back.

It was the first and last time that Christmas roast goat, a regional delicacy, was prepared at our house.

LLEGARON YA LOS REYES

An Argentine Folk Song

Llegaron ya los Reyes eran tres:
Melchor, Gaspar y el negro
    Baltazar.
Arrope y miel le llevarán,
un poncho blanco de alpaca real.

El niño Dios muy bien lo agradeció.
Comió la miel y el poncho lo abrigó.
Y fue después que sonrió
y a media noche el sol relumbró.

The Kings arrived, they were three:
Melchior, Gaspar, and black
    Balthasar.
Syrup and honey they brought Him,
A white poncho of real alpaca.

The Christ child was grateful.
He tasted the honey and the poncho
    swaddled Him.
And then He smiled,
And at midnight, the sun was bright.

Argentine Matambre

 FLANK STEAK ROLL

Knowing that Estela Herrera is a great cook, we begged her to give us this recipe for the *matambre* she mentions in her story.

THE MARINADE

2 2-pound flank steaks, butterflied

1 teaspoon minced garlic

1 teaspoon dried thyme

3/4 cup good quality red wine vinegar

Marinate steak one day in advance: Trim away all gristle and fat from the meat. Lay one steak, cut side up, on a non-reactive 12 × 18-inch pan. Sprinkle it with half the vinegar, half the garlic, and half the thyme. Place the second steak on top and repeat the process. Cover the pan and refrigerate overnight.

THE STUFFING

1 pound fresh spinach or Swiss chard

Water for blanching

2 tablespoons olive oil

2 medium onions, sliced into rings 1/8-inch thick

8 to 10 medium carrots, peeled, sliced and cooked al dente

4 large eggs, hard-boiled and quartered

1/4 cup fresh parsley, finely chopped

1 teaspoon dry red chile, crumbled

1 teaspoon salt, preferably coarse

Wash and trim the spinach or chard. Discard the stems and blanch the leaves.

In a small frying pan, heat the oil and cook the sliced onions slowly until translucent (about 10 minutes).

Lay the steak end to end, seasoned side up, overlapping them about 2 inches. Pound the joined ends together to seal securely. Spread the spinach leaves evenly over the meat and place the carrots on top, laying them in a parallel row along the length of the meat, across the grain. Arrange the eggs on top and scatter the onion rings. Sprinkle the entire surface with the parsley, chili and salt.

Carefully roll the steaks along the grain into a long, thick cylinder. Using a 10-foot-long piece of cotton twine, tie one end around the roll about 1 inch from the end and knot securely. Holding the twine in a loop near the knot, wrap the remaining length around the steaks about 2 inches from the edge of the roll and feed it through the loop. Pull the twine tight to keep the loop in place. Repeat until the roll is completely tied in loops at 1-inch intervals, then bring the remaining twine across the bottom of the roll to the first loop and tie it securely.

COOKING THE ROLL

1 quart beef stock, preferably homemade, plus enough water to cover   *20 to 30 pounds kitchen weights*

Preheat the oven to 375 degrees.

Place the steak roll (*matambre*) in a casserole or roasting pan big enough to hold the meat snugly. Pour the stock over it, adding enough water to cover the roll entirely. Cover the pan tightly and place in the middle of the oven for 1 hour. Remove the roll from the pot onto a cutting board or platter and place the weights on top, allowing the juices to drain off for about 5 hours. Refrigerate until cold. Serve thin slices as a cold hors d'oeuvre accompanied by a green salad.

Makes 10 to 12 servings

Argentine Matambre

Gary Soto

Gary Soto grew up in Fresno, California. He has written twenty-seven books for adults and young people, including Baseball in April *(Harcourt Brace),* Living up the Street *(Dell),* Too Many Tamales, *and* Chato's Kitchen *(both from Putnam). He lives with his family in Berkeley, California.*

ORANGES AND THE CHRISTMAS DOG

FOR CHILDREN, Christmas means the arrival of gifts. At age ten in sloppy clothes and misshapen clown's shoes, I wanted my share. I was greedy for something, anything, even the oranges and pens my stepfather's mother pressed into our arms. My brothers and I could have hopped the fence and gotten free oranges from our neighbors. But I figured why make a face about an expected gift, especially since my stepfather—drunk in his recliner, his head hovering over a TV tray stamped with dead presidents—would have bellowed about our ungratefulness.

Children expect gifts, and if Baby Jesus shows up, that's fine, too. As a Catholic fourth grader at St. John's Elementary School, worried for the poor and the children of Biafra, I wanted Baby Jesus to be born, swaddled, sung to, adored, celebrated . . . all that. But then—and I'm sorry to say this—I just wanted to get my presents. That year I ruined all the expectation of Christmas by tearing tiny holes in the wrapping of my three gifts. With the roving eye of a surgeon examining stomach guts, I probed into the bright wrapping. In the box there was a jigsaw puzzle, in another a sweater, in the third a rifle. I could see that the rifle didn't cock like the more expensive toy rifles, the kind the rich kids would get. Mine was just a length of hard plastic to point at my neighbor Johnny or my little brother, Jimmy, or even my own head, and sputter, "*Tutututututu*, you're dead!"

My older brother, Rick, was outside trying to kill time until Christmas, which was two days away, a slow drip of minutes like a leaky faucet. He had to do something to keep his mind off the presents.

"I know what I got," I told Rick as I walked toward him on the frost-hard lawn. In fog-shrouded Fresno, the neighborhood of ancient houses was dead. Only kids or really dumb people would venture into that chilling scene. Maybe we were both.

"You peeked, huh?" he said. He was eating free oranges from the neighbor's house. "You stupid!" He knew that I had wrecked my happiness. Now I would have to wait an entire year, until next Christmas, before that overwhelming yearning for presents possessed me again.

"I got a rifle," I mumbled.

"I picked it out," Rick said.

"You're lying."

"It's a green rifle." The final slice of his orange went into his mouth.

Then I thought that maybe this mean brother of mine did pick it out, and had chosen a cheap one so that Mom could buy him better presents. I felt angry as a ferret. My breath shaped into a fist in front of my face. But before I could act on my anger, the neighbor's shamefully underfed dog walked over. His fur was like the dirty carpet under an overturned chair. Without a collar or the tinny chime of dog tags, the mutt appeared naked. His ribs clearly showed.

"Watch this." Rick pulled an orange from his jacket and clawed it. He peeled off a slice and fed it to the dog.

"He likes 'em," he said.

The dog closed his mouth around the orange slice, letting it rest there for a moment. As his furry chin began to churn, a trail of juice leaked from his mouth.

Poor dog, I thought, he's really hungry. I took the orange from Rick and dug my fingers into it, then held out a piece. The dog took a step on the frosty lawn. I wondered if his paws were cold without any shoes. Once I had walked barefoot from the house to the car to get a comic book. Those thirty or so steps hurt. I couldn't imagine having to walk on frost all winter.

Rick left. The dog raised his watery eyes to mine. A groan issued from the cave of his lungs.

"Don't go away," I told the mutt. I dashed into the house and threw open the refrigerator. Wasn't a starving dog an emergency? I pulled open the meat drawer and eyed the bologna, my stepfather's precious lunch. I carefully peeled off a single slice, set it on a piece of bread, and covered it with a second piece. But in my hand, the sandwich lacked the weight that might fill in a starving dog's ribs. Again I scanned the meat drawer: a chunk of hard yellow cheese. I broke the cheese into crumbs and sprinkled it on the sandwich. I considered spanking the bread with mayonnaise, then reconsidered, and hurried outside.

"Hey," I called. The dog had walked partway up the street. He turned his head slowly, then his body, and sat down, paws together. I hurried to him.

"You need to eat," I told him. I shoved the sandwich at his mouth. His nose, black as oil but dry as a leaf, sucked in the smells. He sniffed, then took a small bite. I figured he was so hungry, so tired, that he would eat it slowly, one little bite at a time.

"You're going to be okay," I told him, my hand riffling through his matted fur. He finished the sandwich and I went back inside for milk. What could be better than milk to wash down a sandwich? It took a while to find something other than a cereal bowl. It would bring on Mom's wrath if she found out I was feeding a dog from our dishes. I returned with a soup can brimming with milk. I had to walk slowly, one careful step at a time, the frost crunching like bones under my shoes.

"Where are you?" I called to the dog, who had moved further down the street to Mrs. Prince's house. "You like milk, don't you?" I asked as I got closer.

The dog didn't reply with a bark. He didn't appear any friskier from the sandwich or relieved that someone was concerned. I thought that maybe he would see me as a savior. Wasn't it nearly Christmas? He looked at me with watery eyes, his sadness as ancient as the Nile.

I poked the can under his nose. He sniffed its contents. I poured milk, splash by splash, into my palm and let my new friend quench his winter thirst until his snout was nearly drowned in milk.

"That's good, huh?"

The dog turned away, done with me, fed but maybe unsatisfied, his lifeless tail like a shoestring. I placed the can on the curb intending to pick it up later. But I heard a tap-tap on a window: Mrs. Prince had parted her curtain and shook a finger at me. I waved and picked up the can. I chased after the dog, who loped like a burro, with a slow, clip-clop action of hooves.

We stopped at the corner of Angus and Thomas. The streets were dead in the cold, metal-gray afternoon. The sun would not reach us that day.

"Where do you want to go?" I asked.

The dog looked straight ahead. Then, like a zombie, he crossed the street. I followed, pressing him, "Where are you going? Huh? You're going to get lost!"

I remembered from somewhere—a nature program like *Wild Kingdom?*—that a sick elephant left the herd when it knew it was dying. I was scared. Was this dog pacing out the distance from our block to where he would finally roll on his side, kick his paws into the air, and die?

"You ain't sick, are you?"

I stopped him by hugging him around his neck, warm as blankets. I looked him straight in the eye, my own face appearing on the surface of his wet eyeballs. That scared me even more. I was suddenly part of this dog's life, a picture on the windows of his soul. I knew that animals didn't have souls, or so the nuns taught, but I could see, however briefly, that my presence held meaning for this dog. His tail began to wag.

I rubbed his back, building up the heat of friction. I patted him and ran my hand over his head, slendering his eyes. Two more teary drops leaked away the picture of my face.

"Let's go back home." If I had been meaner, I would have cursed the owners of this dog, a family of renters who had shown up one day. They lived two houses from us, and we were told to stay away from the three sickly kids with broomstick bodies. My mother thought they might have TB.

"Come on," I begged the dog. "Let's go back. I got another sandwich for you."

I turned him around and pushed and prodded him to return to our block, which had nearly disappeared in the fog. It looked unfamiliar, like an altogether different town, with different people, different cars, and if the doors were flung open, a whole set of kids I didn't know.

I walked alongside the dog, whose pace had quickened, as if he were in a hurry. Had he been human, he might have looked at the watch on his wrist. He started to run, not fast but fast enough that I threw the soup can to the curb and broke into a jog. I couldn't worry about littering.

"You're going to get lost!"

The dog cut erratically across lawns and into the street, heedless of the occasional cars, sinister headlights frisking the leaf-strewn street. He slowed for a moment, then trotted up someone's lawn and onto the porch. I didn't dare climb the steps. My mom always warned us to stay out of other people's yards, advice I usually ignored on my block. But here, in this strange place, I stayed on the sidewalk. I was cold. My nose was red and I jumped from foot to foot.

"Come on," I whispered to the dog on the porch. He sat only a brief moment and then climbed down the steps and made his way to the backyard. He acted as if he belonged there, the family pet instead of a stray.

"No! Don't go over there!" I yelled.

The dog didn't look back. I thought he was on his way to his grave, the place to lie down in fog. And when the fog cleared, he would be gone. I stood on the sidewalk, not sure what to do. A giant sycamore dripped water on me. Cold worked into my bones. I rubbed my hands together, gathering up heat, waiting for him to reappear. As I stood there, I recalled how in second grade I had asked my mom if there was a chance that one day I might become a saint. I had just returned home from St. John's Elementary and I wanted more than anything to be holy by feeling for the poor, who were so plentiful. I don't remember her answer.

I figured here was my chance to approach sainthood, my chance to walk alongside the dog until it was time for him to die. I must have waited on the curb, freezing, for two hours. Finally, I eventually ventured into the backyard, whispering, "Come on, boy. Come on!"

I raised my eyes to the windows. At any moment a large man would come out yelling for me to go away. He would have a gun or a stick to whack sense into me. That's when I discovered that not only was the dog gone, but I was no saint because I was ready to give up so soon. I felt ashamed, then mad. When I returned home, the dog was back on his porch. He had cut through the yard, leaving me standing in the cold.

"You're bad," I scolded the dog, who didn't even seem to recognize me. He sat among orange peels and ripped-up newspaper. One of the broomstick kids came out. His skin was nearly transparent, and his eyes were sunken.

"Leave my dog alone," the kid said.

I did. I returned home, stiff from the cold. After I stood over the floor furnace, I wandered into the kitchen. It was 4:30 and dark outside. A few orange porchlights cut through the fog. The dark descended on us. Soon Mom was home from work, followed by our stepfather, who took his place in his recliner, the TV coloring the walls. After dinner, Pearl showed up with gifts of pens and oranges. Christmas was two days away, but we were allowed to open one present each. Pearl looked on, face heavily rouged, smiling and hoping that we would pick hers. And we did. I tore into that poorly wrapped present and smiled up at her, for wasn't it Christmas, a time to be appreciative, like a dog? I dug my fingernails into the oranges. Their mist and scent atomized that moment when I knew that I was no saint. I fit not one but five slices into my mouth. I chewed, churned the juicy pulp, and swallowed for Pearl, such a happy woman, who waited for me to clear my throat and say once again, "Thanks, Pearl, these oranges are really, really good."

Orange and Cilantro Salad

This salad is a refreshing foil for the spicier dishes on our menu.

10 medium navel oranges, peeled
    and sectioned, cut into chunks
1 medium red onion, thinly sliced
½ cup chopped fresh cilantro

juice of 1 lime
2 tablespoons olive oil
1 teaspoon honey
salt to taste

Toss oranges, onion, and cilantro in a salad bowl. Whisk together remaining ingredients. Pour dressing over salad and toss.

Makes 8 servings

Jicama, Pomegranate, and Watercress Salad

There are many traditional Mexican *ensaladas de Navidad*, but we love to make this one because the dark-green watercress and the bright-red pomegranate seeds reflect the colors of the season. The jicama adds a nicely refreshing crunch. Pico de Gallo is a Mexican seasoning available in many supermarkets. The ingredients are salt and an exquisite blend of powdered chiles. This hot, red powder can be sprinkled over everything from mangos to corn on the cob. But be careful! It can be *muy picante*!

juice of 1 lime
3 cups jicama, cut into matchstick
slices (about one small jicama)
¼ teaspoon Pico de Gallo seasoning,
or powdered chile, to taste

2 bunches watercress
a few dashes of olive oil
²⁄₃ cup pomegranate seeds (about
½ medium pomegranate)

In a bowl, squeeze the lime juice over the jicama, then sprinkle on the Pico de Gallo and toss well. In a separate bowl, toss the watercress with a little olive oil. Arrange the dressed watercress on a serving dish, pile the jicama in the middle. Then working over the dish, so that juice drips down into the salad, scoop the pomegranate seeds out of their shell with a spoon, and drop them onto the watercress in little mounds.

Makes 8 servings

Esmeralda Santiago

Esmeralda Santiago is the author of two memoirs, When I Was Puerto Rican *(available in English and in Spanish from Vintage) and* Almost a Woman, *and a novel,* América's Dream. *She lives in Westchester County, New York.*

A BABY DOLL LIKE
MY COUSIN JENNY'S

I WAS EIGHT and I wanted a baby doll like my cousin Jenny's, with pink skin and thick-lashed blue eyes that shut when we lay her down to sleep. The doll had no hair, but its plastic skull was traced with curved lines that ended in a curl on her forehead, painted chestnut. It was the size of a small baby, its chubby arms and legs slightly bent, its tiny fingers open to reveal a hand with deep furrows and mounds. I loved the way it smelled, rubbery sweet, and its round little body with a tiny, perfectly formed navel above its belly fold. The baby doll had no penis, but there was a little hole in her bottom, at the end of the crease on her back that defined her tiny flat buttocks.

Christmas was coming. I could tell because the songs on the radio were about how much the singer needed a drink, or about how his woman had left him alone and miserable through the holidays. There were other songs, about the *parrandas* who went from house to house playing music in exchange for a piece of roasted pork or a *pastel* wrapped in a banana leaf or a shot of

87

ron cañita. The neighbors tied red crepe paper around hibiscus and gardenia bushes, hung crocheted snowflakes along the eaves of their tin roofs, displayed flaming poinsettias on their porches. The smells of Christmas floated from every kitchen: ginger and cloves, cinnamon and coconut, oregano, rosemary, garlic. Thick, gray smoke curled from the backyards, where pigs roasted, their skin crackling and sizzling to the scratching of *güiros*, the strumming of *cuatros*, the plaintive *aguinaldos* about the birth of Jesus on Nochebuena.

While Nochebuena was the adult's holiday, El Día de los Tres Reyes Magos was for children, the day we'd wake to find the presents they delivered after traveling thousands of miles by camel. Papi helped me compose a letter, which I worked on for days, laboriously copying it over and over until there were no spelling errors and my request was clear. "Dear Three Magi: I have been good this year. You can ask Mami and Papi if you don't believe me. I would like a baby doll like my cousin Jenny's, with blue eyes that close. I hope you like the water I left and the grass for the camels. Have a good journey. Sincerely, Esmeralda Santiago (Negi)."

Papi gave me a sheet of paper from the ones he used to write his letters and poems and let me borrow his pen, which meant I couldn't make mistakes because the ink could not be erased. My sister Delsa asked me to write a letter for her.

"Ask them," she said, "for a baby doll like the one Jenny has."

"But that's what I want," I said.

"We can both get one and pretend they're sisters."

But I didn't want Delsa to have a doll like mine, so in Delsa's letter, I wrote: "Dear Three Magi: I have been a good girl this year. I would like a doll, but not like the one you're giving Negi, so that we won't get confused. Sincerely, Delsa Santiago." I didn't ask Papi to check the spelling, and I wrote her letter on a piece of notebook paper. When Delsa complained, I told her the Three Magi would know she hadn't written it if the letter looked too fancy, since they knew she was only six years old and couldn't write very well.

The days between Nochebuena and El Día de los Reyes were the longest two weeks of the year. Right in the middle, we celebrated New Year's with noisemakers and songs that no longer despaired of lonely holidays but hoped for better days ahead. Mami and Papi gave us cloth pouches filled with nuts and raisins, and we were allowed a sip from the *coquito* Mami made, which tasted sweet and coconutty and made our heads spin if we sneaked more when our parents weren't looking.

The night before the Three Magi were to come, my sisters and brother and I searched for the freshest, most tender blades of grass to leave in our shoes for the Magi's camels. We placed the shoes under our beds, the toes sticking out so that the Magi would see them. We cleaned out empty tomato-sauce cans and filled them with water from the drums at the corners of the house. Then we lined them up by the door, my letter in front of my can, and Delsa's in front of hers. The other kids complained that we had an advantage because we could write, but Mami convinced them the Three Magi knew what each of us liked, even without a letter.

I woke up while it was still dark. Two shadows moved around the room carrying bundles in their hands. I closed my eyes quickly. It must be two of the Magi, I thought, while the third stays outside with the camels. Next time I woke it was daylight, and Delsa was squealing in my ear. "Look Negi, look! I got a baby doll just like Jenny's!"

I scrambled out of bed, looked under it, found a flat rectangular package under my shoes. It didn't look wide enough to hold a baby doll. It was a box with a colorful painting of a racetrack divided into squares and stiff horses in various positions around it. Papi saw my disappointment, and asked, "Don't you like it?" His face looked worried, and Mami came and stood next to him and looked at me sadly.

"I wanted a doll," I cried, "like that one." I grabbed the doll from Delsa's arms, and she grabbed it back and ran to a corner of the room.

Mami and Papi looked at each other. Mami knelt and hugged me. "You're a big girl. This game is for a big girl. Dolls are for little kids."

"But I want a doll," I sobbed. She looked at Papi, who took my hand and walked me to the yard. Across the room, Delsa undid the baby doll's dress, its pale pink skin glowing under her brown fingers.

"I'm sorry," he said. "I couldn't afford two dolls, and she's younger . . ."

"What?"

"I'll get you a doll for your birthday."

"What happened to the Three Magi?"

Papi looked at me, his eyes startled, his lips pursed into a tight O. "I'm sorry," he said and hugged me.

Forty years later, as I prepare for my American Christmas, I remember that embrace, the soft, moist feel of a just-shaved cheek, Papi's slumped shoulders. I search aisles of toy stores, looking for the perfect baby doll for my daughter, who doesn't like dolls, telling myself all little girls want one. Knowing this little girl still does.

Arroz con Coco

When Esmeralda's mother, Ramona Santiago, makes this dessert, also known as *arroz con dulce*, she mixes the cinnamon sticks and some of the cloves from the spice infusion with the rest of the ingredients. Those of us lucky enough to get a piece of cinnamon or a clove in our portion of *arroz con dulce* prolong the pleasure of Christmas by sucking on the spice.

1-inch piece fresh ginger, sliced in half	enough water to cover rice
4 sticks cinnamon	3 cups unsweetened coconut milk
15 whole cloves	1 cup white sugar
4 cups water	1/2 cup seedless raisins
1 cup short-grain rice	1 cup unsweetened coconut flakes
	powdered cinnamon

Combine ginger, cinnamon, cloves, and water in a saucepan. Bring to a boil, lower heat and simmer for 30 minutes. Remove chunks of ginger, cinnamon and cloves. Soak rice in water to cover for 30 minutes. Drain and add to the spice infusion. Simmer, covered, for 10 minutes. Add coconut milk and sugar. Simmer, covered, for 10 more minutes, stirring frequently. Add raisins and cook 5 minutes more, continuing to stir. Stir in coconut flakes and cook 5 minutes more.

Spread mixture evenly in a rectangular (9 × 13-inch) glass mold. Allow to cool. Sprinkle powdered cinnamon to taste. Refrigerate. Serve cold.

Makes 12 servings

Judy Vásquez

We discovered this poem by Judy Vásquez in a Christmas issue of the newsletter
El Boricua. *The poem commemorates the passing on of the tradition of Christmas*
pasteles; *the title refers to* jíbaros, *the rural dwellers who have become a symbol
of Puerto Rican culture. Ms. Vásquez is a poet and writer and the founder/director
of Kikiriki, a Puerto Rican folk-dance group. Her autobiographical poem reminds us
to be thankful for little miracles, like snow in El Paso—the city where she now lives.*

JÍBARISMOS

Last night
wrapping *pasteles*
my daughter asked
"Why do we have to do this?
It is hard work!"
"To keep culture alive," I said.
Water it
let it root
deep
like mami and grandma did
on Nochebuena, holidays
wrapping it
like the *pasteles* in banana leaves.

That night
two large pots of *masa* and meat
too big for the fridge
slept on my porch.
I was up three times
worrying
thinking it might spoil.

¡Olvídate!
Nature too
keeps the *jíbarito*
alive and well in El Paso.
In the morning

a blanket of snow
cooled the pots on the porch.

This evening
green smoke

steams the window glass
bits of *achiote* burst
to the rhythm of Tito Puente
the *pasteles* dance in the pot.

Gioconda Belli

Gioconda Belli is a Nicaraguan writer living in the United States. She is the author of three novels and five books of poetry. Her work has been translated into eleven languages. Two of her works, the novel The Inhabited Woman *(Warner Books), and* From Eve's Rib *(Curbstone Press), a collection of poetry, are available in English. She is currently at work on a memoir to be published by Alfred A. Knopf.*

A CHRISTMAS LIKE NO OTHER

IT HAD BEEN a strange day. Christmas shopping in the heat. God, it was hot. The store was crowded. People yelling and screaming, bumping into each other. There were only a few good stores in Managua, so I didn't have much choice but to stay where I was until I had selected all the toys for my four-year-old daughter. Christmas shopping is always bad, especially for a person who leaves everything for the last minute, but that day was even worse. Maybe I was getting sick. I felt feverish.

At the cash register, Don Jorge must have sensed my claustrophobia. "Leave the presents with me," he said. "I'll have them wrapped for you. You won't have to wait in line." I didn't think twice. I accepted his offer. He owned the store. He'd known me since I was a child. Impeccably dressed in beige linen, he extended his hand to take my bag. It was a Christmas miracle. One of the Three Wise Men had come to my rescue disguised as Don Jorge.

As I stepped out of the store, the sun was setting. In Nicaragua, the sunsets are always spectacular. It must be a thing of the tropics: thick clouds

95

sprouting in the skies like gigantic pink spirals of cotton candy. The magentas. I walked to my car wiping the sweat from my forehead. Such heat in December was not normal. At the end of the rainy season, the weather is usually moderate. Strong trade winds cool the air. But on that December 23, the air was still. Too still.

I walked down the shop-lined street. Every store window was sprinkled with artificial snow. Winter scenes were everywhere: reindeer, miniature snow-covered villages, Santa Claus sliding down a cardboard chimney— Christmas symbols of another culture and a different climate. But it didn't matter. Even in the tropics, snow was a requisite for a dignified Christmas. Even if it had to be make-believe snow.

At home, I threw myself on the bed. I didn't even feel like playing with my daughter. It was too hot. I turned the air-conditioner on full blast. Maryam climbed on top of me, trying to catch my attention. My head ached. My body ached. I was restless. It didn't feel like Christmas. It felt as if it were going to rain, the way it feels before a tropical storm when the wind dies and the air turns dense, heavy, oppressive. Something bad was going to happen. I knew it. I didn't want to think about it very much, but I knew it. I can sense things.

I got up and called Alicia, the maid, to come and help me move Maryam's crib into my bedroom.

"It's too hot," I said. "She'll sleep better with air-conditioning."

"So very still," Alicia said. "Do you think it might rain? Have you ever heard of rain at Christmas time?"

Together, we gave Maryam her bath, her dinner.

"Santa is coming tomorrow, Mummy. Isn't he?"

"That's right, Baby. When you wake up it will be Christmas Eve. At midnight, Baby Jesus will bring your presents. When you wake up, you'll have many presents right next to your bed. Sleep tight now. Tomorrow is a big day."

She had just gone to sleep when my husband, Mariano, arrived. While we had dinner, he poked fun at the potted palm I had decorated as a Christmas tree. I had to admit that it looked a bit sad and dismayed, unaccustomed to its costume of lights and glass balls. But I had refused to put up a plastic pine tree. I wasn't going to join the collective madness.

At ten o'clock, I heard a rumble. I was standing next to Maryam's crib, patting her back to quiet her light sleep. I expected to feel the earth move, but nothing happened. Just the sound. The rumble deep inside the earth, under my feet. A quake without a quake. Just the rumble.

I came out of the room, alarmed, scared. My husband was watching TV in the living room.

"Did you hear that?"

"What?" He gestured for me not to disturb him. He didn't like to be disturbed while he was watching TV.

"Something bad is going to happen," I said. "We'd better leave the keys next to the door when we go to sleep. I don't want to have to look for them in the dark."

"Don't get all worked up. You know how you are."

Yes. I have a flair for vividly imagining catastrophes. Once the idea gets into my head, my mind becomes a flowing stream, alive with tragic visions, detailed pictures in which I am always the one to be buried under the rubble, the one who has to jump from the balcony of the hotel in flames. When I am on an airplane, I struggle with my mind, forbidding it to conjure images of the plane crashing. Not only can I envision the crash, but I go as far as making up the newspaper headlines that will appear the following day, imagining the row of photos of dead crew members on the front page, just under the big picture of the wreckage.

"This time I'm right," I said. "I know it."

I went around the house removing my favorite vases from the tables and putting them on the floor. I placed the house keys next to the door after double locking it, just as we did every night.

I could have been wrapping Maryam's presents, I thought. It would have helped to distract me. It had been a mistake to leave them at the store. I missed the ritual of sitting on the living room floor late at night, wrapping gifts. Now there were no presents to hide in the trunk of the car.

At eleven o'clock everything was quiet. Maybe I was wrong, after all. Maybe it was just the heat, the stillness, that had made me nervous.

I left my handbag and the flashlight next to my bed.

The next thing I knew, I was on my knees hanging on to the bars of my daughter's crib. I had been thrown from the bed in my sleep.

———

IT'S PITCH DARK. There's no electricity and the earth is shaking so hard I can barely get on my feet without falling. The noise is deafening. The earth is rumbling, growling like a furious beast. Mariano appears next to me. I'm trying to get Maryam out of the crib, but I can't keep my balance.

"Get her out! You get her out! Let's get out of here!" I hear myself screaming. He finally manages to hold on to her. We run for the front door. The walls of the house are creaking, the whole world is creaking, being jolted, rocked with incredible force. The plants hanging in the interior garden are crashing against one another, spilling soil and shards of pottery. Broken glass from the windows is scattered over the floor. We run across the dirt, mud, glass.

Wrapped in a towel, Alicia is running out too, shouting God Almighty, the Holy Trinity, Holy Mary, Mother of God. Thank God the keys are next to the door. I turn the key in the lock, but the door won't open. The earth keeps shaking and we can't get out. I curse my husband's obsession with security. Every window in our house—even the glass walls of the interior garden—has steel bars. We are locked inside a prison. My hands are trembling. I scream that I can't open the door. Mariano puts our sleepy child in my arms and starts kicking it. The frame has been shaken out of line and it's stuck. He kicks harder and finally, as he pulls the handle with all his desperate might, the door opens a crack, just wide enough for us to escape. As we rush out to the sidewalk, a wall comes crashing down across the street. Everyone who lives on our block is outside. Some of them are screaming. Some are holding on to one another. The pavement is waving, undulating like an ominous black snake.

AND THEN, as suddenly as it had started, the shaking stopped.

All of us out on the street began to move in slow motion, as if we were unsure how to gauge the size of the blow we had been dealt. As I turned to look around, clutching my daughter, clinging to my husband, I saw the sky. A cloud of dust floated over the horizon above the roofs. The shimmering sky was brown-red, lit like a second sunset, eerie, apocalyptic, as if the sun had dropped right in the center of the city. The full moon, enormous, glowed red, too. This is the end, I thought. It's the end of the world. Judgment Day. Soon the trumpets will sound, summoning us to God's presence.

Someone shouted, "Managua is on fire!"

The neighbors were milling around. "Are you all right? Is everyone in your house all right?" Everybody on our block was accounted for. I was still carrying Maryam. My arm was numb, but I didn't want to put her down. She clutched me silently. My legs ached. I couldn't trust the ground I was standing on. It was a terrifying feeling, as if we were all standing on the back of a crazed creature that was trying to shake us off.

THE SOUND STARTS again. Somewhere deep in the earth, monsters are demolishing their enormous castle. It's sheer panic this time. We are wide awake. We are already out of doors. We have nowhere to run, nothing to distract us from the horrifying crescendo of the earthquake's rumble. We can see our houses jump as if they are weightless. The utility poles sway like palm trees in a hurricane. Power lines swing back and forth over our heads. Glass breaks. It's pandemonium. Sirens scream in the distance. The whole city rocks like a ship in a storm. I hold my daughter. I bury her head in my chest. I cover her ears. I pray for it to stop. My husband starts screaming, "Let's go! Let's go!" But there is nowhere to go. No other solid ground to stand on. Nowhere to be safe.

THE SECOND EARTHQUAKE didn't last as long as the first. When it stopped, it was after midnight. Alicia left to look for her family. An hour or two passed. Aftershocks kept rocking the ground. People began to set up camp on the sidewalk, pulling out mattresses, blankets. We decided to spend the rest of the night inside the car. I had read somewhere that a car is the safest place to wait out an earthquake. We parked a block away from our house, next to an empty lot.

Suddenly, the weather changed. A cool wind began to blow. I wrapped Maryam in the crocheted cloth I had pulled from our dining table in our rush to get out of the house. My teeth were chattering. My husband looked dazed, absent, behind the wheel. We tried listening to the car radio, but there was nothing. Just static. I prayed for the night to end. Was this only happening in Nicaragua or was the whole world breaking apart, shattering to pieces? I wanted to know. I longed for the dawn. It would be Christmas Eve, and there would be no presents for my daughter.

AT DAYBREAK we drove to my parents' house. My brother had come by during the night to check on us and to tell us they were safe. As we arrived, we saw one of my mother's uniformed maids coming out of the house with a silver breakfast tray, neatly laid out with a lace cloth. She headed for the empty lot next door where my mother sat, quite composed, on an aluminum beach chair. She was even wearing lipstick. It was a scene worthy of Fellini.

My father was gone. As soon as it had become light enough to see, he had set off to find out what was left of his business. My mother hadn't been able to stop him.

Friends and neighbors stopped by my mother's improvised living room, everyone anxious to tell where they had been when the quake hit, what they had done, what they had thought. It was like a horror story competition. But there was humor in the telling. Humor is always present in Nicaraguan tragedies. Maybe that explains why we have been so resilient, surviving a history worthy of Sisyphus.

A recently married friend lamented with dramatic gestures the loss of a beautiful Mexican dinnerware set, a favorite wedding present. "There's nothing left of it," he whined. "Not a saucer, not a cup. Nothing! Nothing!" Under different circumstances, I would have laughed, but now, I found his story endearing. Listening to so many tales of loss, I understood that it was not a matter of money. There were tears for an old rocking chair that had been in the family for generations, for pre-Columbian vases, a record collection, a book. There was the story of a man who had died in the second quake because he had gone back into his house to recover his toupee.

After a few hours my father came back, covered in dirt, his face gaunt and pale. He told us the city was in ruins. Losing control, he covered his face and collapsed onto a stool, sobbing like a child. By that time we had come to understand the enormity of what had happened. Managua had been built in the old Spanish style: colonial houses with thick adobe walls. It crumbled in the Richter 7.5. Then the market caught fire. Fireworks for the holidays,

Christmas lights, bales of cotton to be used as fake snow. Poor wiring. A short circuit and everything went up in flames. The blaze traveled from block to block, unrestrained. The debris in the streets blocked the fire trucks. Now there was nothing left downtown but twisted and smoking rubble. Our city was no more.

"What about Don Jorge's store?" I asked.

"It burned," my father told me. "It burned to the ground. So did ours. I've nothing left."

"Yes, you do," I protested, trying to help him out. "The new store, the one that just opened. That area is still standing."

"People are beginning to loot. Everything will be stolen." He began to cry again.

My father was a hardworking man. I had to get him to do something. I couldn't stand to watch *him* crumble, too.

"Let's go there first," I said. "Let's go now and take out whatever we can. You'll have something you can use to start over. We can take the truck."

Early that morning a friend of my father's had sent a truck from Léon to help us move out of Managua. People were leaving town, seeking refuge in nearby cities. The death count was rumored to be twenty thousand. There were no resources available to recover the bodies. No running water. No electricity. Pipes had burst. The main turbine at the power plant had been damaged. It would be days before these services could be re-established. Corpses would decompose.

"Let's take the truck and go right now," I insisted.

It didn't take my father long to react. I knew he would. My husband was sitting with my mother, still dazed. Maryam was playing with the other kids, running around the empty lot. She couldn't grasp what had happened. She wouldn't understand until later, when she'd wake up in a strange house on Christmas Day, with no presents next to the bed. Then I would have to explain. I would have to tell her the truth. Now, though, she was happy. It was a big party, all the adults hanging out on the empty lot, talking and talking, letting the children run loose around them. I asked my mother to look after Maryam, then climbed into the truck with my father and the driver.

I will never forget driving through Managua that morning. The sidewalks in the badly hit neighborhoods were lined with coffins. Simple wooden boxes, big and small. The stunned, disbelieving faces of the living. The Christmas decorations mocking us. The broken store windows with their still-smiling Santas. The make-believe snow. The fallen lights. It was as if some cruel God had played a bad joke on us. Why did it have to happen right at Christmas? My head was buzzing from lack of sleep. I couldn't believe what I was seeing. It had taken only one minute to throw our lives so wildly off course, to shatter all our certainties. I remembered my premonitions of the day before. This time, what had really happened was worse than anything I could have imagined.

THE SHOPPING CENTER was deserted. All the big windows were broken. There was glass everywhere. The building itself had sustained the impact, but inside the open stores, all the merchandise had been strewn over the floors. Shelves had collapsed, scattering their contents.

Next to my father's brand new shop there was a mattress store. The damage inside was minimal. Mattresses don't break when they fall. Posters on the wall offered a free life-size doll with the purchase of a full or queen bed set. Some of the dolls still sat upright on the mattresses; others lay tumbled in garish positions, their legs up in the air, rocking with the aftershocks—so many I had stopped counting. Because they were so big—my daughter's size, at least—the dolls looked like stranded girls, their blue eyes fixed on some dream landscape that kept them smiling. I couldn't take my eyes off them as I kept passing the store, carrying merchandise from my father's shop to the truck. It was sad to think of them abandoned there. No Christmas for them, either. No little girl to mother them, to give them a name, brush their hair. There was one I liked the most, a brunette in a flowered baby-blue dress. One shoe had come off. She was lying sideways on the bed. I began to see my daughter's face superimposed on the doll's.

The idea took shape as I walked past for the second, third, fourth, tenth time. We were about to finish carting off all the boxes and bags we had filled. A doll that size would make up for a lot of lost toys. I could just imagine Maryam's face when she woke up. It was a matter of faith. I wanted my daughter to believe in magic for a little longer. I didn't want her to think that Santa had perished in the earthquake along with the city, and I didn't want to have to tell her he didn't live in the North Pole surrounded by hardworking elves who labored all year to fulfill children's wishes at Christmastime. But how could I even think of doing something like that? My father wouldn't approve. Here we were, saving our belongings from the looters and I was considering stealing the neighbor's property.

What would it matter, though? Who would care? I went to the mattress store and moved the doll closer to the door.

"We have taken enough," my father said. "Let's go."

I followed him, looking back at the doll once more. I couldn't do it. Whatever the circumstances, there were things one just didn't do. I climbed back into the truck. Being good wasn't making me feel any better. I felt like a coward. I was trapped in a moral code that was going to deny my daughter her innocence, her fantasy. What could be more important than that?

The driver put the key in the ignition and started the engine. The sound startled me. It made me react. In a minute, I was climbing out of the truck, running into the building, shouting to my father to wait, there was something I had to do. I ran over the broken glass, suddenly exhilarated, knowing because of the way I was feeling that I was doing the right thing. Any mother would do it. My daughter's face, my father's hope, the belief that we would be able to overcome such hardship, were the only things that mattered now.

I grabbed the doll. As I passed the pharmacy, I stepped through the broken glass and pulled out two cans of powdered milk. When I got back to the truck, my father looked at me. I sat the doll on my lap, pulled a lock of hair away from my face and told the driver we could leave. Sometime during the ride back, my father hugged me. His eyes were moist. When the tears began to roll down my cheeks he patted my back. He understood. He forgave me.

A few days later, at my in-laws' house in another city, I watched Maryam on the floor, playing with the doll. She must have sensed my thoughts. She turned to me with the concentration small children show when they have thought about something long and hard, and said, "Mummy, it's a good thing there was no earthquake where Santa lives."

Francisco Goldman

Francisco Goldman grew up in suburban Boston, Massachusetts. He is the author of The Long Night of White Chickens, *which won the Sue Kaufman Award for First Fiction from the American Academy of Arts and Letters and* The Ordinary Seaman *(both Atlantic Monthly Press). As a contributing editor for* Harper's *magazine, he covered Central America in the 1980s. He has been twice nominated for the PEN/Faulkner Award, and is the recipient of a Guggenheim Fellowship. His work has appeared in many other magazines, including* Esquire, *the* New York Times Magazine, *and* Sí. *He is currently at work on his third novel.*

IT'S MAGIC!

MY VERY FIRST MEMORY of life in the United States is a Christmas memory. I was born in Boston, but when I was still a baby my mother took my sister and me back to Guatemala, where we lived in my *abuelo*'s house. We didn't return to Massachusetts until I was nearly four. So, for me, the beginning of memory itself seems to take place in the stone patio of that house in Guate, teeming and visceral as a medieval village square, with Indian servant girls killing and plucking chickens or frying potato chips on the outdoor stove; butterflies drowning in the brimming stone fountain; my first tricycle, which I rode round and round the patio; my fat, black rabbit; all the strong smells, rainy-season mildew and lemon-rind rot.

I have no Christmas memories of that time, though the family photo

album does preserve a relic of a seasonal rite, a studio photographer's Día de la Virgen de Guadalupe portrait of me, my sister, and my cousin. A majority of the population of Guatemala is pure Mayan, so every December 12, to celebrate the Virgin of Guadalupe's Day, Guatemala City's non-Indian, mainly mestizo, middle-class children have the custom of dressing as *inditos* in honor of La Virgen, Patrona de las Américas, Queen of the Indians, the brown Virgin, who appeared in 1531 to the Indian Juan Diego on a Mexican hillside.

There we are, little Frankie and Barbie Goldman and our cousin Leonel Molina, posed before a studio photographer's backdrop of an Indian hut, all of us dressed in the ceremonial *traje* of K'iché Maya Chichicastenango, the boys with little charcoal mustaches drawn on their faces. It was Abuelita, on behalf of herself and her husband, who mailed this token religious holiday cheer to my Jewish father in Boston, writing on the back, "Here your two little Indians. [sic] With our very best wishes for a Merry Xmas and a Happy New Year . . . Francisco y Hercilia." What could my father have thought when he opened the envelope and looked at that picture for the first time? It was possible that his family might never live with him again. Now, here were his little Catholic mestizo "Indians." *Oy vay!* Merry Xmas.

Within the next year, my sister and I contracted tuberculosis. This saved us from having to grow up in Guatemala (a country that I still ferociously love-hate and feel compelled to visit as frequently as I can—though it terrifies me to think what might have become of me had I grown up there). My mother took us back to Boston, in part for the better medical care, and my parents resolved whatever had temporarily separated them. My father was waiting for us in a suburban ranch house. I don't think that the rest of us— mother, sister—had lived there before. It was Christmas. I was nearly four.

I remember a big orange-and-black steam shovel, so big and tall it practically came up to my waist. The shovel could be manipulated by chain and lever. I stood by this toy in a happy bewildered state, while Daddy grinned down at me. There must have been a Christmas tree. For some reason, my memory always situates this scene where it seems unlikely to have occurred, in an unpaneled corner of the basement, in front of the terrifying, rust-hued, monster robot that lived down there: a roaring furnace.

I spoke more Spanish than English. I've heard a tape recording from that time, in which I recount a trip to the zoo, sounding like the inventor of Spanglish, my accent strongly *chapín*. In little more than a decade, that accent would become just as thickly Bostonian—so much so that during my freshman year in college my advisor confessed that he'd thought I had a speech impediment until he heard my father talk. I always thought Daddy sounded just like Tip O'Neill, with the same Boston blue-collar crustiness and integrity.

My father's family had fled the Russian pogroms. He and his youngest siblings were born in the United States. Two decades older than my mother, my father was born in 1910. He became an American Jew. He was never very religious, though his sense of Jewishness is strong—essential to who he is, despite the fact that he married a Catholic. In our family, it was Christmas that we celebrated, not Hanukkah. We celebrated my mother's holidays and of course all the American holidays, and every Passover we went either to my uncle Hy's or my auntie Mimmie's or auntie Lee's.

Still, I've always thought of Christmas as my father's holiday. Not that he was in any way undignified about it. He never, for example, would have thought of accompanying my mother, my sister, and me to midnight mass. Christmas for my father, I think, had almost an Old Testament meaning, because to him it marked the return of his family from their "unholy" wanderings—the return of his son! I don't think I've ever seen my father looking so happy as he does in a photograph taken that first Christmas, holding his wheezing, tubercular, Daddy-besotted little boy in his arms.

Our Christmases were celebrated, for the most part, in the American suburban way. It may be because my family in Guatemala owns toy stores, but the Molinas, like many middle- and upper-class Central Americans and Mexicans, celebrate Christmas in the American suburban way, too: Santa Claus, toys, strong family sentiments and nostalgia, tree, eggnog, and (on the religious side) nativity, crèches, church, the beautiful Bible story, and occasionally the feelings of holy wonder and tenderness. But Christmas is about children, and for many of us it's really the mystery and magic of a child's world that is celebrated.

All countries have their folkloric traditions. My mother, a schoolteacher, liked to make a big deal of these. Her enthusiasm strikes me now as incredibly sweet, but it embarrassed me then, when I was growing up, just wanting to be another "American." Guadalupe Day, dressing like Mayas, eating tamales and drinking *atole*, trailing behind the *tica-toca-tic* sounded out on a turtle-shell drum—these things were a lot of fun for my mother and her Spanish Club students. They appeared every year on local public television to show New Englanders how the holiday was supposed to be celebrated in Guatemala—and probably it was, before shopping malls and the universalization of American consumer Christmas. With her Irish and WASP and even Jewish students all dressed like Mayas, my *mamita* would cradle a hollow turtle-shell drum in one arm and with a stick beat out the *tica-toca-tic* rhythm, holding a pretend *posada*, imitating Mary and Joseph's journey as they went from house to house asking for shelter on their way to the manger of Bethlehem. In the TV studio or wherever the Spanish Club Christmas party was being held that year, they'd just march around a bit and then stop to eat. But in Guatemala, you were supposed to be given tamales, hot chocolate *atole*, and other treats at the houses where you stopped, like Christmas carolers.

My mother retired from teaching this year, and it has been several years since she appeared on TV with her Spanish Club students. But whenever I go home, I see the turtle shell propped high on a bookshelf in the den, the drumstick resting inside its hollow cavity. This funny turtle shell—with its aura as a famous TV prop—now retired.

At home, we didn't do that—march around with the turtle-shell drum. Though I remember my father, high on eggnog, performing an antic Bolivian handkerchief dance. Sometimes we had relatives over for Christmas Eve, though usually my parents invited friends: my mother's Latin American friends, my father's old Jewish neighborhood friends, who were so close to family we called them aunts and uncles. My sister and I would be forced into playing duets. My sister played the violin brilliantly. I faked and huffed and honked along on the clarinet so badly that, finally, I'd bite my reed in half, pretend it had been an accident, and then act dismayed to discover that there were no more reeds left in my clarinet case.

Sometimes, we'd make a short Christmas Eve trip to the house of one of my mother's Latin American friends to admire their Nativity crèche. They had an antique porcelain Christ child in its cradle, a family heirloom from colonial times, which had traveled with them from Bolivia to Boston. I remember standing around the precious doll singing carols.

But Christmas was my father's holiday, and so was Halloween and just about every other holiday except Easter. Perhaps it was because he'd married late in life and was so thrilled to have children. One Halloween while I was lying in bed I was suddenly awakened by a knocking at my window, where I saw a hideously masked face, and I screamed and *screamed!* The face vanished. Still crying, I gaped at the night-blackened window and heard the smash of rattled aluminum, then a deep groan outside in the backyard. Daddy had fallen backwards on the ladder. He was laid up for about a week after that with a hurt back. He was lucky he hadn't broken it.

I will never forget one Christmas moment. It must have been the very next year after that first Christmas Eve in Massachusetts. My father was holding me in his arms. It was snowing. And we were standing outside our front door. My father excitedly pointed at the sky and shouted, "Can you see them?! Hear them? See them, Frankie! Santa and his reindeer!" And he said it with so much conviction that I finally saw them, too, flying through the sky and the snow, high in the sky above the rooftop of the O'Donnell's house and the trees on the hill behind—Santa and his reindeer! I've never forgotten that sight. Who could ever forget seeing something like that?

(Gabriel García Márquez once told an interviewer that a key to his fabulous art is the understanding that "there is nothing more convincing than conviction itself.")

More than three decades would pass before I would find myself again being persuaded in a similar way, filled briefly with that same sensation of hallucinatory enchantment and excitement as I listened to a similar-sounding conviction—and I understood, then, exactly what it was my father had given me that first time. I was visiting a friend in southern Spain for Christmas. His little daughter, Rosie, and I were out on the porch, just after dusk, gazing down the hill at the lights and the Mediterranean beyond, the night sky a beautiful luminous blue with a silver moon and the stars coming out. Rosie, in her nightgown, was explaining, her voice emphatic with the excitement of what she'd just figured out: how it is that Santa Claus and his reindeer can fly. "People say it's impossible," she said. "They say it's impossible that he can fly." And she widened her eyes indignantly. "But they don't understand!" Rosie shook her head as if it were all just so obvious, and held out her hands in an exasperated gesture of *can't you see how simple it really is?* "It's magic," she said. "He can fly, because he's magic. That's why it's called magic. It's magic!"

Hot Chocolate Atole

THICK HOT CHOCOLATE

Atole is a hot cornmeal drink, and it can be flavored with chocolate or cooked fruit. If you're lucky enough to live near a market that caters to Mexican-Americans, you'll have no trouble finding the ingredients. The Mexican chocolate comes in discs individually wrapped in paper. It's already loaded with sugar and, depending on the brand, it's flavored with cinnamon, nutmeg, or crushed almonds. Be sure to look at the ingredients. Ibarra brand, which is imported from Guadalajara, is very pure—just sugar, cocoa, almonds, cinnamon, and lecithin. Abuelita is another common brand. It's made in Mexico but distributed in the United States by Nestlé, so it's not hard to find. It melts well but lacks the flavor of almonds. What you decide to add to this recipe will depend on what's already in the chocolate you use.

2 cups warm water

2 heaping tablespoons masa
    harina *(corn flour—
    not cornmeal)*

2 cups milk

1 disc *(about 3 ounces) Mexican
    chocolate (If you can't find real
    Mexican chocolate, you can
    substitute 3 ounces of sweetened
    chocolate, and add* $1/4$ *teaspoon
    each of cinnamon and nutmeg
    and a dash of almond extract.)*

In a blender, mix the corn flour and water until smooth (but see note, below). Transfer to a saucepan and bring to a boil, whisking constantly. Lower heat and simmer, for about 5 to 10 minutes, stirring to prevent lumps, until the mixture begins to thicken. Add the milk, raise the heat, and continuing to stir, bring the mixture almost to a boil. Lower the heat a little to prevent the milk from boiling, add the chocolate, and continue to whisk until all the chocolate is melted and the mixture is smooth. Simmer for 10 to 15 minutes more. The *atole* will be thick and creamy. Serve in mugs.

NOTE: Nowadays, many markets in Mexican-American neighborhoods sell "instant" *masa harina*, which eliminates the risk of lumps. If you can find it, you can skip the blender. Just mix up the corn flour with the water in your saucepan using a whisk.

Makes 2 generous servings

PEDIDA DE LA POSADA

Asking for Lodging

FOR NINE DAYS leading up to Christmas, the *posadas* are celebrated, re-enacting Joseph's search for an inn where Mary could give birth to the baby Jesus. There is a procession from house to house with candles and a manger scene, usually carried by children. Outside each house, the group sings Joseph's verses, begging for shelter, while inside, the host, who takes the part of the innkeeper, sings back his objections. When the door is opened at the end of the song, the group is invited in for refreshments—tamales, hot chocolate, and other treats. And there is often a piñata to break and sweets for the children.

San José
　En nombre del cielo
　Os pido posada
　Pues no puede andar
　Mi esposa amada

Saint Joseph
　In the name of Heaven
　I beg you for lodging
　For my beloved wife
　Cannot walk.

Casero

> Aquí no es mesón;
> Sigan adelante.
> Yo no puedo abrir;
> No sea algún tunante.

San José

> No seaís inhumano;
> Tennos caridád.
> Que el Dios de los cielos
> Te lo premiará.

Casero

> Ya se pueden ir
> Y no molestar.
> Porque si me enfado
> Los voy a apalear.

San José

> Venimos rendidos
> Desde Nazaret.
> Yo soy carpintero.
> De nombre José.

Casero

> No me importa el nombre;
> Déjenme dormir,
> Pues que ya les digo
> Que no hemos de abrir.

San José

> Posada te pido,
> Amado casero,
> Por solo una noche,
> La Reina del Cielo.

Innkeeper

> This is not an inn here,
> So keep going.
> I cannot open my door;
> You might be lazy vagrants.

Saint Joseph

> Don't be inhuman;
> Have pity on us.
> God in Heaven
> Will reward you for it.

Innkeeper

> You had better go
> And don't disturb us.
> Because if I get angry
> I'll beat you up.

Saint Joseph

> We are worn out,
> Coming from Nazareth.
> I am a carpenter.
> My name is Joseph.

Innkeeper

> I don't care what your name is;
> Let me go back to sleep.
> I already told you,
> We're not opening the door.

Saint Joseph

> I ask you for lodging,
> Dear innkeeper,
> Only for one night,
> For the Queen of Heaven.

Casero	*Innkeeper*
¡Pues si es una reina	Well, if it's for a queen
Quien lo solicita,	You are asking,
Cómo es que de noche	Why does she travel at night,
Anda tan solita?	So alone?
San José	*Saint Joseph*
Mi esposa es María	My wife is Mary.
Es Reina del Cielo,	She's the Queen of Heaven
Y madre va a ser	And she's going to be mother
Del Divino Verbo.	Of the Divine Word.
Casero	*Innkeeper*
¡Eres tú José?	Are you Joseph?
¡Tu esposa es María?	Your wife is Mary?
Entren, peregrinos,	Enter, pilgrims.
No los conocía.	I didn't know who you were.
San José	*Saint Joseph*
Dios pague, señores,	May God repay
Vuestra caridad,	Your kindness, señores,
Y así os colme el cielo	And the heavens
De felicidad.	Heap happiness upon you.
Casero	*Innkeeper*
Posada os damos	Lodging I give you
Con mucha alegría,	With much joy.
Entra, José justo,	Enter righteous Joseph.
Entra con María.	Enter with Mary.

Victor Martínez

Victor Martínez is a native Californian. He is the author of A Parrot in the Oven *(HarperCollins), for which he received the 1996 National Book Award for Young People's Fiction.*

BARRIO HUMBUG!

As a boy, my Christmases were dreary reminders that my family—no matter how colorfully one wants to paint it—was poor. Until my father discovered the Lions' Club cheap-toy giveaway, what my brothers and I each got for Christmas was a rubber-banded bushel of dime-store socks and a pair of can't-bust-'em jeans to weather both winter and summer. Once, I got a plastic tyrannosaurus and, in the panic attack that followed, almost hyperventilated, believing God had definitely made a mistake—toys like that go only to rich kids!

Either way, my mother claimed we were lucky. In Mexico, she'd tell us, one doesn't expect a multigear bike, just some fruit and clay animals stuffed into one's shoes. Mexicans, she said, aren't soulless and corrupt like people in the United States, where there's so much to give away that we need two full-blown Christmases: one for the faithful minions of Jesus and another for those who just want to get drunk and receive gifts.

My mother was a wise woman, and still is, for that matter, but I was twenty-four by the time I figured out what she meant. That Christmas Eve, my sister Estela and I sat in our cousin's living room waiting for the twelve o'clock hand to turn. Around us, like wolves over the carcass of a deer, sat my cousin's children, breathless, waiting. My cousin wasn't wealthy—what Chicano family from Fresno, California, is? But he could, as they say, "rub the poor man's magic lamp" (which meant he could pinch pennies).

When the clock finally cranked twelve, a twister suddenly whirled into the room, snarling and licking at our hair. Actually, it was the kids, their little faces contorted with greedy enthusiasm, their chubby hands snatching at gifts as if they were afraid the toys would scurry away.

Kids barely out of their baby teeth became as predatory as great whites. The walls of the house practically collapsed from the frenzy of their feeding. My sister and I shivered with an icy fever from the cold greed. Those kids didn't just "open" their presents, they eviscerated them to judge—in a calculating second—what the hypereffluvia of their imaginations had been whipping up for months. Then they'd give off this low, almost caustic snort of disappointment. Obviously their gifts were not as phantasmagorically splendid as their fantasies. But then, maybe the next gift was! So immediately they gouged into another package.

There is a no more tortured landscape than the face a child makes when he hasn't gotten what he wanted for Christmas. Even this disappointment lasted only an instant, however. After gathering their own stash about them, they instantly decided what they really wanted was someone else's stash! That's when the fighting began, the sudden clap across the jaw, the stubborn pout, the grip on another's Tonka trucks, now undesired, now just weapons to be flung.

I stumbled away from my cousin's home a scorched man; I decided I'd never spin the wheel of Christmas commerce again. From that day on, I resolved, I would punch Santa on the nose (figuratively speaking, of course) whenever we crossed paths. I would remain unimpressed when my eyes happened to gaze upon a celestially baubled Christmas tree blazing magnificently at me from a department-store window. Any manner of rapture for this evergreen symbol, I believed, could only be purchased with a vacant heart, a heart that no longer listened to the howling, unexpressed agony of obliterated forests.

Furthermore, I felt free to explain to anyone who'd listen, we Chicanos were no better in this regard than anyone else. Corporate America had its hand buried to the elbows in our pockets. Ours was no innocent idyll of *posadas* and festive dinners. Here in America, I'd rant, we take as big a bite out of the earth's rump as the next glutton.

If you disagreed, I'd confront you with this: "Ask yourself how many times you've heard politically earnest Chicano parents say, 'Well . . . the kids like it. It's for the kids.' And how many times have you seen the eyes of those same parents, who marched their dogs dead for equal rights, start twinkling on and off, red and green, when Christmas rolls around? We're as sentimental about this holiday as we are about El Movimiento. So every year," I'd go on, "we shovel billions to corporations selling happiness inside a flame-red wrap. Why? Because we sense that, although we're responsible for them, our children don't really belong to us. They belong to the nightmare schools that educate them, to the fright-wig friends who influence them, to the pop-and-schlock slot machine that passes for culture in this society!" I'd be very eloquent.

As you can probably imagine, riffs of moral umbrage of this sort didn't exactly endear me to family and friends, especially since I didn't have any children of my own. I became as welcome at family gatherings as a blistering rain on a papier-mâché parade, and despite the tradition that declares that hospitality cannot be refused without risking serious astral repercussions, people quit inviting me to Christmas dinners altogether.

Happily, one learns with age—as I'm sure my mother, who had the wise soul of an ascetic Buddha, learned that no one wants a mealy bug in their geraniums. The gravity of my need to dematerialize myself wasn't as weighty as my need to be among people. After all, I came from a family of seven brothers and five sisters, and I wasn't used to being out in the cold. To be the Grinch at Christmas is to sled solo.

In the end, a little attitude adjustment served me well. As you may have guessed, I eventually succumbed to the glittering vortex of Christmas. I, who once touted my egalitarian cynicism to the stars, became a hypocritical wuss. And what of it? Christmas is a disease cured only by the death of one's fake enthusiasm for self-containment. If you want to know the truth, I like gleefully munching on cinnamon *buñuelos* and unabashedly drinking spiked eggnog under the mistletoe, and—call me a wimp—but I enjoy muddying my hands with *masa* every year for the customary tamales.

I'm not about to change back into that young, cynical spoiler who almost had his pessimistic butt driven from the family hearth. Because, at bottom, that is what Christmas is all about: family. For one day in a year that may have brought many disappointments, my family gets together and we talk, fight, relive past crimes inflicted on ourselves and others, and then we forgive. The world is out there, and we are in here; not alone, but together.

Mexican Buñuelos

CINNAMON FRITTERS

These delicious, crisp fritters take time to prepare, but they're well worth the effort. If you've never made them before, you may have to practice a little to get the dough thin and even. But don't worry too much if you can't make perfect circles. They'll be delicious whatever their shape.

3 1/2 cups flour	*4 tablespoons lard or solid vegetable*
1 1/2 teaspoons baking powder	*shortening*
1 tablespoon sugar	*1 large egg, beaten lightly*
1/2 teaspoon salt	*1 cup lukewarm water*

Mix together flour, baking powder, sugar, and salt. Gradually blend in shortening, bit by bit, working it into the dough until it disappears. You can use a pastry cutter or two knives to accomplish this, or just crumble the shortening and work it into the dough with your fingers. Make a well in the mixture and, using a fork, gradually work in the egg, then the warm water.

The dough will be soft and a little sticky. If it sticks to your fingers, dust the surface with a little more flour as you turn it onto a floured board. Knead, working the dough hard, for about 10 minutes, punching it down and folding it over, pounding it with your fist. (This may sound like a lot of work, but it's actually fun—even therapeutic!) Cover the dough with a towel and allow it to rest for at least 30 minutes.

Pinch off little pieces of the dough and roll into 1-inch balls. Flatten the balls into circles with the palm of your hand, then roll into circles about

6 inches in diameter. Gently stretch the circles around the edges with your fingers. The circles should be paper thin.

Pour about 1½ inches of oil into a skillet and heat until hot but not smoky. Next to the stove, have a tray or platter covered with a double layer of brown paper or paper towels. You can test the heat by sprinkling a drop or two of water into the oil to see if it bubbles up. Drop the circles into the oil one at a time. Hold the circle under the oil with a slotted spoon just until it begins to turn golden, then flip over and brown the other side. The *buñuelos* will tend to turn darker as they cool, so don't overcook. Drain the *buñuelos* on the paper, then sprinkle with the cinnamon-sugar mixture.

Serve at once. Or, allow to cool thoroughly and then store in a closed tin.

Makes about 18 6-inch buñuelos

THE SYRUP (OPTIONAL)

1 cup dark-brown sugar or piloncillo

3 to 4 cinnamon sticks

1 cup water or orange juice

1 tablespoon anise seed or 12 star anise

Sometimes *buñuelos* are served piled up and covered with syrup. If you decide to use the syrup, eliminate the cinnamon-sugar. *Piloncillos* are little cones of dark sugar found in Mexican markets, but brown or even granulated sugar will do. Put all the ingredients into a saucepan and cook, stirring over medium heat until the sugar melts. The syrup can be made in advance and reheated.

Easy Buñuelos

After days spent perfecting our *buñuelo* technique, Joie's sister, Jacqueline Davidow, offered to get us an "authentic" version of the recipe. She told us that her friend and colleague, Monica Gutiérrez, brought the most exquisite *buñuelos* to work during the holiday season, and she was sure she could be persuaded to share her secret. Imagine our chagrin when we read these ingredients! These fritters are not quite as light and crispy, but they're a lot less labor intensive.

1 package small flour tortillas, very fresh

shortening for frying
cinnamon and sugar to taste

Cut each tortilla into quarters. Deep fry in shortening that is very hot but not smoking. Remove just as tortillas turn golden brown. Drain in a colander lined with paper towels. Mix together 2 parts cinnamon to 1 part sugar in a flat pan. A cake pan works very well for this. Dip each hot, fried tortilla in the cinnamon-sugar mixture to coat it. Shake off the excess and voilà!

Each tortilla makes 4 buñuelos

Tamales Dulces

 SWEET TAMALES

Tamales, filled with chicken, cheese, or meat, make a great meal all year long, but sweet dessert tamales are a special Christmas treat. These, filled with pineapple and raisins, are a specialty of Mercy E. Lara's Saguaro Café in Tolleson, Arizona. But you can also try them with other fillings, such as shredded coconut, almonds, pine nuts, candied fruit, or bits of guava paste, and add spices such as cinnamon, nutmeg, or anise.

1 bag corn husks
4^1/$_2$ cups masa harina
   (corn flour or coarsely
   ground cornmeal)
1 tablespoon baking powder
1^1/$_2$ tablespoons salt
^{1}/$_2$ cup granulated sugar
^{1}/$_2$ cup brown sugar

1 cup shortening (butter, lard, or
   a combination of the two)
2^1/$_2$ cups beef broth (canned or
   homemade)
^{3}/$_4$ cup raisins
1 medium can (20 ounces) crushed
   pineapple

Soak the corn husks in a bowl of warm water for at least 15 minutes. They should be soft and pliable. Be sure to remove any remaining bits of corn silk.

While the husks are soaking, place the *masa harina* in a large mixing bowl. Add baking powder, salt, both sugars, and the shortening, and mix well. Add the broth and mix again thoroughly, until the batter is smooth and free of lumps. Stir in the drained raisins and pineapple.

Stack your very clean, larger corn husks beside your mixing bowl. Take a few of the husks and shred them into little strips for tying. Place a husk in your left hand and place 2 large tablespoons of batter in the middle of the husk. Now roll the husk over the batter, as though you were rolling a cigarette, fold the ends in, and tie with a strip of husk. You can vary the size and shape of your tamales as you like but the filling must be well covered.

In a steamer large enough to accommodate all the tamales, add about 3 inches of water. Add the tamales, bring the water to a boil, and steam for about 40 minutes. Since these tamales are meatless, they cook quickly. The finished tamales should be solid, but the filling should be soft and moist.

Makes 2 to 3 dozen tamales, depending on the size

Sandra Cisneros

Sandra Cisneros was born in Chicago in 1954. Internationally acclaimed for her poetry and fiction, and the recipient of numerous awards, including a fellowship from the MacArthur Foundation, Cisneros is the author of The House on Mango Street, Woman Hollering Creek and Other Stories, My Wicked Wicked Ways, *and* Loose Woman. *She lives in San Antonio, Texas, and is currently at work on a novel.*

UN POQUITO DE TU AMOR

WHEN MY FATHER DIED last year, a week before Valentine's Day, a piece of my heart died with him. My father, that supreme sentimental fool, loved my brothers and me to excess in a kind of over-the-top, rococo fever, all arabesques and sugar spirals, as sappy and charming as the romantic Mexican boleros he loved to sing. *Dame un poquito de tu amor siquiera, dame un poquito de tu amor nomás. . . .* Music from my time, Father would say proudly, and I could almost smell the gardenias and Tres Flores hair oil.

Before my father died, it was simple cordiality that prompted me to say, "I'm sorry," when comforting the bereaved. But with his death I am initiated into the family of humanity, I am connected to all deaths and to their survivors: "*Lo siento,*" which translates as both "I am sorry" and "I feel it" all at once.

Lo siento. Since his death, I feel life more intensely.

My father, born under the eagle and serpent of the Mexican flag, died beneath a blanket of stars and stripes, a U.S. World War II veteran. Like most immigrants, he was overly patriotic, exceptionally hardworking, and, above all, a great believer in family. Yet often I'm aware my father's life doesn't count, he's not "history," not the "American" politicians mean when they talk about "American."

I thought of my father especially this holiday season. The day before Christmas 1997, forty-five unarmed Mayas were slain while they prayed in a chapel in Acteal, Chiapas—twenty-one of them women, fourteen children. The Mexican president was shocked and promised to hold all those responsible accountable. The Mexican people aren't fools. Everybody knows who's responsible, but it's too much to wish for the Mexican president to fire himself.

I know the deaths in Chiapas are linked to me here in the United States. I know the massacre is connected to removing native people from their land, because although the people are poor the land is very rich and the government knows this. And the Mexican debt is connected to my high standard of living, and the military presence is necessary to calm U.S. investors, and the music goes round and round and it comes out here.

I have been thinking and thinking about all this from my home in San Antonio, Texas, as fidgety as a person with *comezón*, an itching, a hankering, an itch I can't quite scratch. What is my responsibility as a writer in light of these events? As a woman, as a mestiza? As a U.S. citizen who lives on several borders? What do I do as the daughter of a Mexican man? Father, tell me. *Ayúdame*, help me, why don't you. *Lo siento*. I have been searching for answers. On Christmas, I am reverberating like a bell.

In my father's house, because my father was my father—*Hello, my friend!*—our Christmas dinners were a global feast, a lesson in history, diplomacy, and the capacity of the stomach to put aside racial grievances. Our holidays were a unique hybrid of cultures that perhaps could only happen in a city like Chicago, a bounty contributed by family and intermarriage, multiethnic neighborhoods, and the diversity of my father's upholstery-shop employees.

To this day, a typical Christmas meal at our home consists first and foremost of tamales, that Indian delicacy that binds us to the preconquest. Twenty-five dozen for our family is typical, the popular red tamales, the fiery green tamales, and the sweet, pink tamales filled with jam and raisins for the kids. Sometimes they're my mother's home-made batch—*This is the last year I'm going to make them!*—but more often they're ordered in advance from someone else willing to go through all the trouble, most recently from the excellent tamale lady in front of Carnicería Jiménez on North Avenue, who operates from a shopping cart.

Father's annual contribution was his famous *bacalao*, a codfish stew of Spanish origin, which he made standing in one spot like a TV chef—*Go get me a bowl, bring me an apron, somebody give me the tomatoes, wash them first, hand me that knife and chopping board, where are the olives?*

Every year we are so spoiled we expect—and receive—a Christmas tray of home-made pierogis and Polish sausage, sometimes courtesy of my sister-in-law's family, the Targonskis, and sometimes from my father's Polish upholsterers, who can hardly speak a word of English. We also serve Jamaican meat pies, a legacy from Darryl, who was once father's furniture refinisher, but has long since left. And finally, our Christmas dinner includes the Italian magnificence from Ferrara Bakery in our old neighborhood on West Taylor Street. Imagine if a cake looked like the Vatican. We've been eating Ferrara's pastries since I was in the third grade.

But this is no formal Norman Rockwell sit-down dinner. We eat when we're inspired by hunger or by *antojo*, literally "before the eye." All day pots are on the stove steaming and the microwave is beeping. It's common to begin a dessert plate of cannolis while someone next to you is finishing breakfast, a pork tamale sandwiched inside a piece of French bread, a mestizo invention thanks to the French intervention.

History is present at our table. The doomed Emperor Maximiliano's French bread as well as the Aztec corn tamales of the Americas, our Andalusian recipe for codfish, our moves in and out of neighborhoods where we were the brown corridor between Chicago communities at war with one another. And finally a history of intermarriage, of employees who loved my father enough to share a plate of their home-made delicacies with our family even if our countries couldn't share anything else.

Forty-five are dead in Acteal. My father is gone. I read the newspapers and the losses ring in my heart. More than half the Mexican-American kids in this country are dropping out of high school—more than half—and our politicians' priority is bigger prisons. I live in a state where there are more people sentenced to death than anywhere else in the world. Alamo Heights, the affluent, white neighborhood of my city, values Spanish as a second language beginning in the first grade, yet elsewhere lawmakers work to demolish bilingual education for Spanish-dominant children. Two hours away from my home, the U.S. military is setting up camp in the name of bandits and drug lords. But I'm not stupid; I know who they mean to keep away. *Lo siento.* I feel it.

I'm thinking this while I attend a Latino leadership conference between the holidays. I don't know what I expect from this gathering of Latino leaders, exactly, but I know I don't want to leave without a statement about what's happened in Acteal. Surely at least the Latino community recognizes the forty-five are our family.

"It is like a family," one Arizona politico explains. "But understand, to you it may be a father who's died, but to me it's a distant cousin."

Is it too much to ask our leaders to lead?

"You're too impatient," one Latina tells me, and I'm so stunned I can't respond. A wild karaoke begins, and a Chicano filmmaker begins to preach— There's a season to play and a season to rage. He talks and talks till I have to blink back the tears. After what seems like an eternity, he finally finishes by saying, "You know what you have to do, don't you?"

And then it hits me, I do know what I have to do.

I will tell a story.

When we were in college my mother realized investing in real estate was the answer to our economic woes. Her plans were modest: to buy a cheap fixer-upper in the barrio that would bring us income. After months of searching, Mother finally found something we could afford, a scruffy building on the avenue with a store that could serve as Father's upholstery shop and two apartments above that would pay the mortgage. At last my mother was a respectable landlady.

Almost immediately a family on the third floor began paying their rent late. It wasn't an expensive apartment, something like a hundred dollars, but every first of the month, they were five or ten dollars short and would deliver the rent with a promise to pay the balance the next payday, which they did.

Every month it was the same . . . the rent minus a few dollars promised for next Friday.

Mother hated to be taken advantage of. *Do they think we're rich or something, don't we have bills too?* She sent Father, who was on good terms with everybody. *You go and talk to that family, I've had it!*

And so Father went, and a little later quietly returned.

"I fixed it," Father announced.

"Already? How? What did you do?"

"I lowered the rent."

Mother was ready to throw a fit. Until Father said, "Remember when ten dollars meant a lot to us?"

Mother was silent, as if by some *milagro* she remembered. Who would've thought Father was capable of such genius? He was not by nature a clever man. But he inspires me now to be creative in ways I never realized.

I don't wish to make my father seem more than what he was. He wasn't Gandhi; he lived a life terrified of those different from himself. He never read a newspaper and was naive enough to believe history as told by *la televisión*. And, as my mother keeps reminding me, he wasn't a perfect husband either. But he was very kind and at some things extraordinary. He was a wonderful father.

Maybe I've looked to the wrong leaders for leadership. Maybe what's needed this new year are a few outrageous ideas. Something absurd and genius like those of my father, whose kindness and generosity teach me to enlarge my heart.

Maybe it's time to lower the rent.

Dame un poquito de tu amor siquiera, dame un poquito de tu amor nomás . . . ever since the year began that song runs through my head. My father just won't let up. *Lo siento.* I feel it.

Papá, Buddha, Allah, Jesus Christ, Yahweh, La Virgen de Guadalupe, the Universe, the God in us, help us. *Danos un poquito de tu amor siquiera, danos un poquito de tu amor nomás . . .* just a little bit of your love at least, just a little bit of your love, just that . . .

Piri Thomas

Piri Thomas is the author of the classic memoir Down These Mean Streets *(Vintage) as well as of three other volumes,* Savior, Savior Hold My Hand *(Doubleday),* Seven Long Times *(Arte Público Press), and* Stories from El Barrio *(Knopf).*

A CHRISTMAS TREE

TWO MORE WEEKS and it would come around again. Christmas. The year was 1938. I was ten years old and living with my family in Harlem. Las Navidades was a sacred time for all the devout Christians regardless of color, for it was in honor of Jesus Christ, who had not even known the comfort of being born in a hospital, since there had been no room at the inn. Instead he had been born in a manger in the stable. Popi, who was a death-bed Catholic, would only see a priest when he was ready to kick the bucket, but when anybody asked him what his faith was, he would proudly boom out, "Me, I'm *católico.*"

For kids in El Barrio, Christmas was a time of great expectations and nighttime dreams of a beautiful yellow bicycle with balloon tires or a brand-new pair of ice skates. I dropped hints all over the place hoping to receive at least one or the other. I would write to Santa Claus asking for what I wanted, always sending my best regards to Mrs. Claus with the hope of establishing a better connection. But the truth of the matter was that nobody heard me. We Thomas children always got something, although not exactly what we had asked for. Our brave, tight smiles with the glimmer of a tear were meant to pass as the happy joy of receiving pretty close to what we wanted, but we sure didn't fool Mami, who, in gentle tones, would tell us that we ought to be thankful that we had received something, at least, since a lot of ghetto children had not gotten anything because of the great unemployment. The lines at Catholic Charities were long and not everybody in them was Catholic. The Twenty-third precinct on 104th Street gave out toys to the kids in our community, and then some of the cops proceeded to bust our chops for the rest of the year. La Casita María in El Barrio on 110th Street gave out warm blankets and clothes and bags of groceries and the Heckscher Foundation on 104th Street was there for us, too, and gave shoes and warm clothing to the very poor. Mami gave each of us a kiss and a tight hug and told us we should give thanks to God that our father had had a job at the toy warehouse for the past two years. I smiled in agreement, but with my thoughts I responded, "Sí, Mami, but they don't have yellow bikes with balloon tires and pro ice skates."

Popi's boss was named Mr. Charles. Popi worked as a toy inspector who checked the toys, separating out the damaged ones as rejects. Popi also served with distinction as packer and porter. Popi had told us that his boss considered himself to be a good guy and so at Christmastime he allowed his workers to take home damaged toys as presents for their children. But all the toys Popi had brought home last Christmas were brand-new with the exception of one single reject among them. As it came out years later, Popi, who like many other parents wanted the best for his children, wanted brand-new toys instead of rejects, and had simply put prime-condition toys into a large potato sack and then placed a damaged one right on top, bringing them all home in one sack, which made us kids very happy on Christmas morning. Of course Popi didn't want Mami to know, because she, as a good Christian, would disapprove of any action that smacked of dishonesty.

It was four days before Christmas and we still had not gotten our tree. Popi had waited until he got his few dollars' Christmas bonus and then announced that it was time to buy our tree and asked us who wanted to come. Of course all four kids began to squeal and jump around, using any excuse for creating joy. I looked out the window of the living room which faced the street. The barrio was covered by a soft white blanket of snow that kept falling gently. "Dress warmly," Mami admonished, and in no time at all the four of us looked like Eskimos, complete with warm scarves that swallowed our faces. As we ran out into the dimly lit hallway and noisily descended the stairs two at a time, I heard Mami call down to Popi about not going crazy and spending too much money on the Christmas tree.

The five of us stepped out into a white world of falling snow and muffled sounds. The snow looked good enough to eat. We could make snowballs and then pour on flavored syrup and eat the balls like *piraguas*. Popi exclaimed, "*Vaya* kids, look at all the snow, is this not a most beautiful sight?" We all shivered in agreement. Lots of *familias* with their children were heading toward Third Avenue. We turned the corner on 104th Street and Third and the avenue was ablaze on both sides of the street with millions of multicolored Christmas lights blinking at each other all the way up to 125th Street. Loud-speakers hooked to the outside walls of well-stocked stores blared Christmas songs like "I'm Dreaming of a White Christmas," "Joy to the World," and "Hark the Herald Angels Sing," with commercial breaks in English and Spanish that promised tremendous bargains with 50 percent off and instant credit.

José was anxious to get to the empty lot near Second Avenue, because he had been chosen to be the one to pick the tree. We all entered the huge lot full of all sizes and kinds of trees. Popi led us to where the regular-sized trees were trying to look their scrawny best, and we followed right behind him— that is, all except José, who was nowhere to be seen. Everybody took a point on the compass and frantically went José-hunting. I hoped he had not been kidnapped and held for ransom. Sis ended those lousy thoughts by waving at all of us to come over. We joined her and as she pointed to the more expensive, taller, and fuller trees, there was little José lost in wonder, looking up at one of the tallest and most expensive trees in the lot! I saw Popi's face like he was remembering what Mami had said about not going crazy and spending too much money. We all stared at José, who turned to us with a big grin on his small face and pointed to what from his vantage point must have seemed like a giant redwood straight from California. Popi smiled at little José, and we all followed suit as Popi tried to persuade José that he had to be kidding, trying to steer our little brother toward some Christmas trees more his size, but to no avail. José held his ground without a grin and kept his tiny forefinger pointed at the gorgeous tree of his choice. Popi offered him a delicious hot dog from a nearby stand, knowing that José (and us along with him) loved hot dogs with a passion, but José was determined not to be moved. His little lips started to quiver and his tiny forefinger was getting tired of pointing and just before the first tears formed, Frankie, my sister, and I were practically glaring at poor Popi, who was hung up in the middle with no place to go. Popi did what he had to do and snatched José up in his arms and raised him onto his shoulder and shouted out for José and all to hear, "Hey Mista, how much you want for this tree?" Popi's eyes pleaded with the Negro brother that the price not be too high, so that he could please his youngest child along with the rest of the family.

The brother, who was an old man of about thirty, looked the tree over, lips pursed like he was into a real heavy decision. Popi finally said, "Well, Mista, what's your price?" and added under his breath, "You know, if it's too high, I won't be able to deal with it." I watched everyone closely. Their faces were somber. José had some tears ready just in case the price was out of the question.

"Well, sir, this tree is worth about ten dollars." We gasped. Ten dollars in 1938 was like two months' rent and food for months and months. Rice and beans were about five cents a pound. Popi shook his head grimly and did not dare look straight at José, who was nibbling his upper lip with his lower. "How much do you have, sir?" asked the mista. "I got a five-dollar bill from which I gotta bring home at least two for the Christmas dinner." Popi squatted down to José's size and offered him a whispered deal of how about us getting a smaller tree and José could have a whole dollar all of his own. José just shook his head and pointed his tiny forefinger up at his personal Christmas tree. Popi got up and whispered to the mista, "Say brother, what's the best you can do?"

"Wal, I sez if you don't mind giving me a hand tomorrow night, you got the tree for three bucks. Whatta ya say?"

"Done deal." Popi shook hands with the mista and said, "My name is Juan but I'm known as Johnny."

"My name is Matt," and that was that. Popi gave Matt the worn five-dollar bill and got two bucks in return. José put on one of his famous grins and we all broke out in a victorious cheer.

The five of us struggled through the snow until we were across the street in front of our building at 112 East 104th Street. We were living on the top floor and it suddenly dawned on Popi that the hallway was too narrow and the turns up the steps were even worse. We tried getting the tree into the hallway, but to no avail unless we wanted to scrape the branches clean. By this time a small crowd of neighbors had gathered around us, some of whom stopped to greet Popi and admire José's great choice of Christmas tree. Then the debate began on how in the heck were we going to get that twelve-foot tree up to our apartment, where the ceiling was only nine feet high. Some suggested we bind the tree firmly and squeeze and bend it around the banister. Popi was listening to the suggestions of the men when Mami, full of curiosity, came downstairs and out onto the street where the small crowd had gotten larger. Mami quickly sized up the situation and brightly suggested, "Why don't we pull it up the side of the building to the fifth floor and then haul it in through the front window?" Everybody smiled and agreed that Mami's way was the best, and soon Pancho, who had a small truck, came back with a long strong rope and a small pulley. He and Popi went up to our apartment and quickly secured the pulley to the side of the fire escape and then ran the rope through it to the street below. By this time neighbors were serving hot coffee to whoever wanted some and small shots of rum to those who might be extra cold. Everybody seemed to be extra cold. The tall, full Christmas tree was then tied to the rope and with Popi on the fifth-floor fire escape directing the hauling, Mami took charge below, with Sis and Frankie watching José, who took in the whole scene with a tremendous grin. Tenants appeared on each fire escape and hands from each of the fire escapes carefully helped guide the tall tree upward until it reached the fifth floor without the loss of a single branch. Popi and Pancho pulled the big tree in amidst a mighty cheer that rose up from the muffled street below—the sound of victory brought about by the unity of neighbors.

After all that, the tree did not fit in our apartment. But Popi was not to be defeated, so he measured it carefully and Pancho sawed off three feet, finally making it the right size. Then Mami had us carry the three feet of Christmas tree down to Abuela Santiago, who lived alone but had almost everybody in the building for an adopted family. Mami took some lights and trimmings and went down to her apartment with José so he could be the one to present the tree to Abuela Santiago. We allowed Abuela and José to do most of the decorating, and Abuela blessed us after we finished. I thought that this promised to be a fine Christmas, indeed.

When Christmas morning finally dawned, my siblings and I dashed out of our bedrooms to look under José's tree, which was now brightly decorated with multicolored Christmas lights blinking on and off. Lo and behold, underneath the tree, in full view of the world, was a pair of ice skates just like the pros used, and on closer look, who the heck cared if they were second-hand, fresh from the Salvation Army thrift store? They were professional skates and that was all I cared about. *Vaya,* next year might just bring the beautiful yellow bike with balloon tires. "Merry Christmas," I began to shout and my siblings followed my example. Soon we were joined by happy kids in the hallway stomping up and down the stairs, shouting Merry Christmas and *Feliz Navidad* to one another. *Punto.*

Judith Ortiz Cofer

Judith Ortiz Cofer was born in Hormigueros, Puerto Rico. The recipient of fellowships from the National Endowment for the Arts and the Witter Bynner Foundation, she is the author of a novel, The Line of the Sun *(University of Georgia Press), two collections of prose and poetry,* Silent Dancing: A Partial Remembrance of a Puerto Rican Childhood *(Arte Público Press) and* The Latin Deli: Prose and Poetry *(W. W. Norton), two volumes of poems,* Terms of Survival *(Arte Público Press) and* Reaching for the Mainland *(Bilingual Press) and a volume of stories for young adults,* An Island Like You: Stories of the Barrio *(Penguin). She is professor of English and creative writing at the University of Georgia.*

THE GIFT OF A CUENTO

THIS IS THE STORY of a *cuento* that was given to me once upon a time, and then again. *Una vez y dos son tres.* I was thirteen. It was the year when I began to feel like a Cinderella whose needs were being totally ignored by everyone, including the fairy *madrinas* I fantasized would bring me a new, exciting life with the touch of a magic wand. I had read all of the virtue-rewarded-by-marriage-to-a-handsome-prince tales at the Paterson Public Library and was ready for something miraculous to happen to me: beautiful clothes, an invitation to a great party, love. Unfortunately there was a dearth of princes in my life, and I was not exactly the most popular girl

139

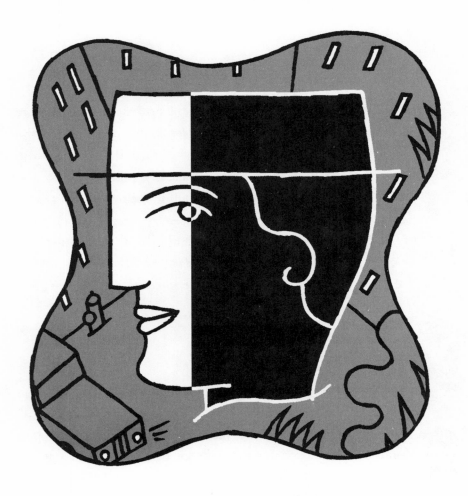

at a school socially dominated by Italian and Irish-American princesses. Also, that year I was in the throes of the most severe insecurity crisis of my life: besides being extremely thin—"skinny-bones" was my nickname in the bar- rio—I was the new girl at the Catholic high school where I had been enrolled that fall, one of two Puerto Rican girls in a small, mostly homogenous social world, and I had also recently been prescribed glasses, thick lenses supported by sturdy black frames. After wearing them for only a few weeks, I developed a semipermanent ridge on my nose. I tried to make up for my physical deficien- cies by being well read and witty. This worked fine within my talkative *familia* but not at school, among my peers, who did not value eloquence in girls—not more than a well-developed body and social status, anyway.

That Christmas season, the *cuentista* of our family entered my life. My mother's younger brother, who lived in New York, was the black sheep of the family, with a trail of family *cuentos* about his travels, misadventures, and womanizing behind him—which made him immensely attractive to me. His arrival filled our house with new talk, old stories and music. Tío liked to tell *cuentos*, and he also liked playing his LPs. My mother and he danced to merengues fresh from the Island—which he seemed to be able to acquire before anyone else, and which he carried with him as if they were precious crystal wrapped in layers of newspaper. He was the spirit of Navidad in our house, with just a hint of the Dionysian about him. Tío enjoyed his Puerto Rican rum, too, so his visits were as short as the festivities, because his bache- lor habits eventually wore down my mother's patience.

Tío must have sensed my loneliness that year, for he took it upon himself to spend a lot of time with me the week before Christmas. We went for walks around the gray city, now decked out in lights and ornaments like an over- dressed woman, and for pizza downtown. He asked me about my social life and I confessed that my *príncipe* had not appeared on our block yet, so I had none.

"Why do you need a prince to have fun?" my uncle asked, laughing at my choice of words. Unlike other adults, he seemed to really listen. Later I under- stood this was how he learned to tell a story. He told me that I had inherited his and my *abuela*'s gift of the *cuento*. And because he was so unlike my other *cariñoso* relatives, who poured the sweet words on us kids without discrimina- tion or restraint (or honesty, I thought), I believed him. I knew how to tell a good story. My mother had warned me that it was Tío's charm, his ability to flatter and to persuade, that usually got him into trouble. I wanted that power for myself, too. The seductiveness and the power of words enticed me.

His appeal had little to do with physical beauty: he was short, dark, wiry, with a Taíno Indian face. But he was generous to a fault, completely giving of himself. Our family dreaded his recklessness, but we also adored him for the many sacrifices he had made for our sake, the good deeds that I heard about, along with the spicy *cuentos* and the gossip about his complex love life.

"I guess I was thinking of Cinderella." I didn't want Tío to think me a child, but I also wanted him to understand me in a way no one else could. I wanted magic in my life. Poised between a sheltered childhood and the yearnings of approaching adolescence, my dreams were hopelessly entangled with fairy-tale fantasies. The prince was the prize I had learned to want from the things I heard and saw around me.

"La Cinderella. That girl has really made trouble for us men," Tío laughed.

We were standing in front of the drugstore where my mother bought her twenty-five-cent Corín Tellado romances—which I also avidly read. My uncle took my hand and guided me inside the store. The rack of Spanish-language *novelas* was a Christmas tree of romance. Passionate couples kissing on every cover.

"See what women read?" My uncle gave the rack a turn, making it go round and round, creating the illusion of a moving picture of embraces and phrases like *"la pasión," "corazón y alma," "besos,"* and the constant refrain of *"el amor, el amor, el amor."*

"Mami reads these," I confessed, "and sometimes I do, too." In fact, it was my job to memorize the titles she had read so she could send me for new ones as they came in.

"They are all Cinderella stories. Every one of them." Tío gave the rack another turn. "The plot is always the same: Poor or unfortunate girl meets rich unattainable man. After many hardships he discovers that the shoe will only fit the girl whose beauty he had not ever really seen because of her rags. If he is an alcoholic, he stops drinking; if he's a miser, he turns generous; if he's short and fat . . ."

"Don't tell me—he gets skinny and tall!"

"Or at least he learns to act as if he were perfect in every other way."

"So what's wrong with that?"

"La vida no es así." My uncle looked uncharacteristically solemn when he told me that the expectations of Cinderella and her female followers were simply not the way life really was for men and women, not even when they were in love.

But I didn't hear him. I knew only that my charming *tío* smelled enticingly of liquor and cigarettes when he leaned down to kiss me, and that he had other vices I could not yet name. But all of that made him alluring to me—the good Catholic girl waiting for life to begin happening for her. He was the mysterious man in one of my mother's *novelas*. I thought he was so much more interesting than my dull, hardworking father and my other male relatives. I didn't know of my *tío's* lifelong battle with alcoholism, or of the throat cancer that would silence his seductive voice forever, before he was much older than I am now.

I remember walking with him past the decorated storefronts of downtown Paterson one evening. My uncle made a game of asking me if I wanted this or that for Christmas: a Thumbelina doll like I had desperately wished for last year? No. I had received a hard plastic doll from one of my grandmothers in Puerto Rico, and my parents had decided that that was enough dolls for me. Only Tío had understood that the Thumbelina baby doll *felt* like a real flesh-and-blood baby. We had gone into the store and held it. He had not bought it for me because that year was one of his *años pobres*, when he was between jobs, holing up or drying out at a relative's apartment somewhere, waiting until he could get together enough money to return to *la isla*. But this year he had money for gifts, he said. Did I want jewelry? We looked at all the shiny baubles in the jewelry store window. No. An *azabache* to wear around my neck to ward off the evil eye? No. I laughed. I was too sophisticated then for such superstitious nonsense.

"Surprise me, Tío."

That week before Nochebuena I stayed close to his magical presence, taking in his masculine appeal, watching women's faces soften when he cast his dark eyes on them, smelling his dangerous other life when he kissed me on the cheek as he said good night and went off like the sleek cat he was to prowl the streets and return in the morning to my mother's kitchen, where his face revealed that he had been *doing* exciting things while the rest of us only dreamed about them.

Mami would frown through her first cup of coffee, then break down in girlish giggles when Tío told us a new joke or *cuento* he had picked up in his wanderings. I gathered these stories in my memory and brought them out during the loneliest times of my life. They nourished and comforted me as they had my mother, who was always hungry for words in Spanish during those first years away from the Island. I had no idea then that my uncle was using his storytelling in a similar way: to trade for attention, time, even affection from others.

"*Mira*, it was like this," he would sit across from my mother at her little Formica table, both of them smoking cigarettes and drinking coffee. "The girl needed attention and I gave her some. I will tell you from the beginning so that you know I am not the scoundrel you think. This is *la verdad, la pura verdad.*"

This phrase was a key to their family joke. Whenever any of my *abuela*'s children started a story with the announcement that it was the pure unadulterated truth, as the old lady always did before one of her *cuentos*, we all knew that it was going to be a good one. A whopper. No holds barred.

"And how was I to know that she was married? All I knew was that her big brown eyes, like my *sobrina*'s there, were beckoning to me from across the dance floor. *Socorro. Ayuda*, they said to me, save me from this lonely life . . ."

"She had very eloquent eyes." My mother might comment in mock seriousness.

"What could I do but respond to her silent cries for help?"

"If someone's eyes cry out for help, *pues*, you must do what you have to do, *hombre*." My mother fell easily into the straight-man role that played such a large part in these entertainments. Their jokes and *cuento*-tellings were more like a little play extemporized by people who knew each other well.

"I did what any man with a heart would have done. I danced a few numbers with her. I bought her a drink. I asked her if she would like me to escort her home. You know the streets of this city . . ."

"Are crawling with criminals!" my mother offered.

"Exactly. Well, that's when she thanked me by telling me that her fiancé was getting off from a late shift at any moment. And . . . well, wasn't that him at the door now? Yes, it was the fiancé at the door, and he looked more like King Kong than any other man I have ever seen. *Hija,* he was covered with black fur from head to toe, and he was so huge that he had to squeeze in through the double doors. Good thing that slowed him down enough so I could end my dance with the lovely *señorita* as quickly as possible."

"But how did you get the egg on your forehead, *hermano?* Did you bump it on your way out?"

"¡Ay, *bendito!* King Kong gave me this little gift. You see there was no back door. And for a big ape, the fiancé moved fast. The only thing I regret is that he wasted a perfectly good bottle of Bacardi by using it as a weapon on my head."

"Maybe it was not all wasted," my mother was giggling and I was, too, by then. "I think it may have seeped into your brain through your pores."

While I listened to my mother and my uncle talk, I saw how all their daily struggles ceased for the time it took to tell the *cuento,* how pleased they were with their own wit, their ability to laugh at disappointments and hurts, and best of all, to transform any ordinary episode into an adventure.

ON CHRISTMAS EVE the family gathered in our living room. My mother and I had polished the green linoleum floor until it was a mirror reflecting the multicolored lights of the Christmas tree which had done its job of perfuming our apartment with the aroma of evergreen. I was wearing a red party dress my mother had let me choose from her closet and a pair of her pumps. I looked at least eighteen, I thought. I put some of Tío's *pachanga* records on our turntable and waited anxiously for him to come through the door with my gift. What I expected it to be was in the airy realm of a dream. But it would, I knew without a doubt, be magical.

It was late when he finally showed up bearing a brown grocery bag full of gifts, a bleached-blond woman on his arm. After kissing his sisters, waving to me from across the room, and wishing everyone *Felices Pascuas,* he and his partner left for another party. My mother and aunts shook their heads at their brother's latest caprice. My feet hurt in the high-heeled shoes, so I sat out the dances and read one of my mother's books. Some time around midnight I was

The Gift of a Cuento 145

handed my gifts. Among them there was an unwrapped box of perfume with a card from my uncle. The perfume was Tabu. The card read: "*La Cenisosa* from our Island does not get a prince as a reward. She has another gift given to her. I heard a woman tell this *cuento* once. Maybe you can find it in the library or ask Mamá to tell it to you when you visit her next time."

My mother thought the perfume was too strong for a girl my age and would not let me wear it. I was disappointed by the gift, but I would occasionally spray on the perfume anyway. I discovered that its wilted flower scent triggered my imagination. I could imagine myself in many different ways when I smelled it. It was the kind of perfume no one else would ever give me again.

I did not find the *cuento* of *La Cenisosa* in the Paterson Public Library, nor in any other book collection for many years. Recently I ran across an anthology of *cuentos folklóricos* from Puerto Rico, and there it was: *La Cenisosa*. In *La Cenisosa* of Puerto Rico, Cinderella is rewarded by a family of three *hadas madrinas*, fairy godmothers, for her generosity of spirit, but her prize is not the hand of a prince. Instead, she is rewarded with diamonds and pearls that fall from her mouth whenever she opens it to speak. And she finds that she can be brave enough to stand up to her wicked stepmother and stepsisters and clever enough to banish them from her home forever. Around the time when I translated this folktale my mother wrote to say that my uncle was dying from cancer of the throat back on the Island where they had both returned years ago. She said that his voice was almost totally gone but not his indomitable spirit. He knew he had little time left to give us the words he wanted us to remember. He had my mother write to me and tell me that he had read my novel and wanted me to know that my stories gave him pleasure. He sent me his *bendición*. I took his blessing to mean that he had accepted my gift of words.

Coconut Flan

This recipe comes to us from Ada T. Rosaly of Ponce, Puerto Rico, the mother of our dear friend, Eileen Rosaly. When Ada visits her daughter in Los Angeles, she is always called upon to bake a flan, which disappears in minutes. Her recipe is virtually foolproof, so even if you've never tried to make flan before, you will be able to impress your friends with this one. The ingredients are not exactly low in cholesterol, but trust us, it's worth every calorie.

1 cup granulated sugar

6 eggs

1 can (12 ounces) evaporated milk

1 can (14 ounces) coconut milk

1 can (14 ounces) sweetened
  condensed milk

1 tablespoon vanilla extract or
  1 shot of rum or brandy

To caramelize the pan

Pour the sugar into a square or round flan mold or cake pan about 9 inches in diameter and 3 to 4 inches deep, and cook over low heat, agitating constantly to prevent scorching. When the sugar begins to bubble, remove the pan from the heat and turn it so the caramel glaze covers the bottom of the mold evenly. Set aside to cool.

To prepare the custard

Preheat oven to 350 degrees.

Lightly beat the eggs, then continue to beat the mixture as the remaining ingredients are added. Beat until well blended. Pour the mixture through a strainer into the prepared mold.

Place the mold into a larger pan filled with ½ to 1 inch of hot water, so that the water comes about half way up the side of the mold. Bake 45 to 50 minutes or until a toothpick inserted in the center comes out clean.

Remove from the oven and allow the mold to cool on a rack. To unmold, dip the mold in warm water before inverting it onto a serving platter.

Makes 8 to 10 servings

Luis J. Rodríguez

Luis J. Rodríguez grew up in South Central and East L.A. He is the author of the award-winning memoir Always Running: La Vida Loca, Gang Days in L.A., *as well as several volumes of poetry. He has been the recipient of a Lila Wallace– Readers' Digest Writer's Award and a Lannan Fellowship. He is also the publisher of Tía Chucha Press, a Chicago-based publishing company specializing in poetry.*

COLORS BREATHING THEMSELVES INTO THE BODY

For Diego Rodríguez

SOUNDS OF Trío los Panchos or Augustín Lara rustled through the wood-paneled room. Christmas at Diego's house glistened with pine needles on a tree, flickering lights on all the branches, and multicolored gift-wrapped boxes heaped in a corner. What I knew about holidays, I had learned from Diego, my half-sister Seni's husband. He was the energy igniting every room, the center of every festivity, the court jester of Los Rodríguez.

Diego was a second father, the other man to guide us. He made sure the children visited parks, took in a drive-in movie, or had a night out at a local diner. When all was gloom, he was light. When all was cruel, he was kind. I don't ever remember Diego angry; he was perplexing sometimes and tough—never angry.

First the cells mutate into a constellation of malignant stars, dividing and replicating, corrupting and influencing—a malfeasance of genes that industry, smog, cigarettes, and chemical-laden foods have blessed us with, palpitating beneath the tissues, birthing and killing at once, like colors breathing themselves into the body.

For a brief period, our family was homeless. It was after the bank foreclosed on our house in Reseda, where we lived for a year as one of the first Mexican families in that part of the San Fernando Valley. My father had lost his job, gone bankrupt, and everything had been taken away. The family returned to South Central L.A., the area of Los Angeles where we first landed after leaving Ciudad Juárez, Mexico, when I was two years old. There were no homeless shelters for families in those days. We slept in the living rooms of *comadres* and friends, taking turns going from one household to another; never in one place for more than a few nights. At one point, my mother was determined to take her children back to Mexico—without my father, if necessary—rather than stay in L.A. with nothing to our name. We made it as far as the inside of Union Station before she changed her mind, her face drenched in tears.

After that, we moved in with Seni, sharing her small two-bedroom apartment in Monterey Park with Diego and their two young daughters. There were eleven of us there at one time, including Seni's family, my grandmother Catita, my parents, and their four children. The children slept on blankets strewn about the living room. There were good times. But there were terrible times. Constant arguing; storming out of rooms, banging of doors. My brother Rano and I crept out of the house into the streets. I was about eight years old. A child could easily disappear between the shouts.

One night, Rano and I came home after dark. There were police cars parked outside our building. Neighbors stood on the lawn and driveway. We went inside to find my nieces and sisters crying. There was blood on a wall. A burly policeman was taking notes. Seni, following a particularly heated argument, had stabbed Diego with a nail file. He was okay. In fact, he decided this was a good time to take the kids to the park while the rest of the family calmed down. So we went along, Diego's arm heavily wrapped in gauze.

We lasted about a year there. Diego tried to keep Christmas alive, even when there were no toys to pass around. Somehow, we weathered all the turmoil. One Christmas, our family received a big bag of groceries, including a turkey, and an allotment of toys from a Catholic charity. Each child had at least one toy to call their own. I was so excited, I broke the little plastic submarine the first day.

On L.A.'s East Side, families were spread out beneath the smog blanket ensnared by the San Gabriel Mountains. The deadly exhalation of every car in the city lingered there. Winds carried the venom, creeping through back windows and air vents. Corridors of industry—the smelters, the rolling mills, the packing sheds, the refineries, the assembly lines—propelled the brown halo across this Valley of Death, which was known for gang violence, but it might as well have been known for the "industry drive-bys" that claimed even more lives.

Cancer, long linked to this polluted environment, struck home. My father died of stomach cancer in 1992. My sister Gloria's daughter had a form of bone cancer. Gloria was diagnosed with lupus and other related ailments. And Diego got hit particularly hard.

The L.A. basin had one of the largest concentrations of industry after the Rhineland. Only Chicago had more. When you think of L.A., don't just think about Mickey Mouse or Melrose Avenue or Muscle Beach; think, too, of the other side of town, of blast furnaces, bucket shops, the odorous funk of Farmer John's slaughterhouse. Think of cancer growing like prickly cactus in a desert. Think of Diego.

THE AIR WHISTLES JAZZED each morning to the worm-worm belly of refineries and factories that consumed generations of *familias* from Michoacán, Guerrero, Durango, Chihuahua, Sinaloa.

Diego began at the paint factory as a gofer. Everyone liked Diego. He made jokes in a terribly accented English, but he spoke with a confidence that sometimes clarified better than words. He eventually learned English, but for years it was a word or two at a time. There was a period when he called everyone "Sugar." Cigarette ash followed him everywhere he walked.

He worked better, smarter, and with greater grace than anyone around. Soon he moved up into positions at the plant where brown skin and strange idioms normally found no home; but Diego, his brashness not a tactic but an authentic song, kept bettering his betters. He learned the chemical composition of paint, how it could change before the eyes, how light falls into a place of colorlessness and allows an inner shade to glow. After a few years, Diego became mixer and creator, the man behind new and complex tones that soon graced the rooms of children and the dens of other working men with a hybridity of hues that danced inside his bones like neon.

ONE CHRISTMAS, when I was about twelve years old, Diego brought out my first new bike. My parents had bought it for me. It had been hidden in the closet; I never suspected a thing. The bike was a shiny blue Stingray with a black leather banana seat. *¡De aquellas, ese!* The coolest thing. For a long time, I had envied other kids their low-riding cycles. But we never seemed to have any money. I had started a paper route and was using a beat-up ten-speed that I had found somewhere and fixed. For once, I had me a new bike!

That night, I parked the bike next to my bed. I stayed up all night just looking at it. I couldn't sleep. The light of the moon through the window struck the bike at all the right angles. It sparkled and shone. Maybe it was my imagination. I don't recall when I finally passed out, but as soon as morning broke, I was up and riding my bike.

I rode it to a friend's house, where I gently placed it on the lawn. I showed it off, then we went inside the house briefly. When I came back, the bike was gone. Stolen! I couldn't believe it. I ran down the street, looking in yards, down alleys and up and down streets. But it was nowhere to be found. My beautiful bike. Gone.

I didn't know how to face my parents or Diego. I never saw that bike again. I never got another one. I kept on using my old ten-speed to deliver newspapers. But I never forgot that bike. I never forgot how important it made me feel, how solid in the world. I never forgot someone had made the effort to give my life such brilliance, even for too short a while, a brilliance that took me through dark times.

———

Tumors erupted all over Diego's body. There were lumps on his throat, head, and hands; the chemotherapy had destroyed his hair; he looked bloated. All the toxins, tints, smells, shades, and smoke had transmuted, developing and feeding on themselves. No sci-fi flick could even come close. For one last time, Diego sat around with the rest of the family, watching the 8-mm films he had made over a span of thirty years: birthdays, Christmases, visits to the beach, to amusement parks, to Mexico. I was thirty-eight years old; Diego was fifty-four. Till the very end, Diego joked, doing the Cantinflas shuffle through the difficult hours of his days. Even in my most confusing moments, Diego never put me down; he always found something to tease me about.

A few years before he died, long after I had left East L.A. and moved to Chicago, Diego arrived in town for a convention of paint chemists. Holed up at a fancy Hilton downtown, he said he felt out of place. There was a Taco Loco down the street in a dingy section of the Loop. Diego called to see if I could come by and visit with him. But not at the Hilton.

"Meet me at the Taco Loco," he said.

When I got there, a homeless man lay across the sidewalk, a wino asked for change, and Mexican hotel workers waited at a bus stop. Diego, meanwhile, was midway into a taco, his coat and tie removed, his white shirt opened at the neck, and mounds of salsa spilling over his plate. It was the last time I saw him looking healthy.

They buried Diego in a vase of ashes. On the day of the funeral his young granddaughter got upset when the funeral-home workers patted the earth with a shovel.

"Don't bury my granddaddy!" she yelled.

The owner of the paint factory attended the services, emerging from a limousine. Some complained he had no right to be there. Others said the guy truly appreciated Diego. Remembering Diego, they all could have been right.

Diego had a way of obliterating all the grays with laughter, songs, and home movies. I haven't had a Christmas yet without remembering how he called out the name on each present, how he passed them out to eager, empty hands—when Christmas was not so much about things but about remarkable people and the gifts they shared.

Rosario Morales

Rosario Morales was born to Puerto Rican parents in New York City. She grew up in Manhattan and the Bronx and moved "back" to Puerto Rico when she was twenty-one. She writes fiction, memoir, and poetry in Cambridge, Massachusetts. Her work has appeared in numerous anthologies such as This Bridge Called My Back, An Ear to the Ground, *and, most recently,* El Coro: A Chorus of Latino and Latina Poets. *She coauthored* Getting Home Alive *(Firebrand) with her daughter, Aurora Levins Morales.*

I DIDN'T GO HOME (CHRISTMAS 1941)

I HEARD THE ruckus in the hall outside the door to the children's ward, the nurses arguing in their soft, annoyed voices, his voice deep and determined. I knew he was coming to take me home even though I didn't have to leave until the next day. It wasn't even visiting hours. It was Sunday morning. The sun streamed in the windows at the long side of the ward. The bustle of the morning had just died. No more toothbrushing. No more injections or pills. No clatter of dishes and spoons. No embarrassing ordeal of doing it on a pot by the side of the bed. Now I was savoring the calm, lying quietly in the sun, and watching the baby in the glass-enclosed room at the end of the ward laughing at the faces that the little girl with leukemia was making at the poor thing. Soon the lady in the pink-

striped apron would come with toys and puzzles, with books and cards. I wondered what we'd have for lunch.

My father gave me an awkward hug, kissed my cheek, and said, "*Ven, m'hijita. Vente, nos vamos,*" while I lay back on the bed not going, not putting on the blue-flowered dress he pulled out of the grocery bag he was carrying. I looked at him trying to say no and not knowing how. I hadn't had too much practice. I especially didn't like to say no when he was so pleased, so sure he was giving me a treat. He was taking me home for Christmas, away from the hospital where I was lonely and afraid. But I wasn't lonely and afraid. Not even when they wheeled me into the operating room with my eyes wide open staring at the tiled walls, the blinding light, the tanks of gas, the white uniformed people, the awful black mask that cut off all air. "Breathe in," they said when I held my breath to keep the sweet strong stuff from entering my lungs. "Breathe!" Good obedient child that I was, I did, and heard their voices disappear into a dream.

Here in the ward I had more company than anywhere but school. All the grown-ups were polite, and while they never hugged me or kissed me or called me "*nena buena*" or "*nena linda*" they never hit or yelled at me or at each other. I did get scolded for laughing at the kid in the next bed straining on the pot, and when my turn came to strain and cry from the pain, I was laughed at, too. But even so, I didn't want to be cheated out of the twenty-four hours I had left.

Papi looked at my face, worrying. "*¿Qué pasa? ¿Te duele algo?*" "No, Papi. I don't hurt." "Come, then," he said, switching to English, the kind of English I still like, the sharp edges softened by his Spanish accent. "Get dressed and we'll go home and have some *asopao*." But not even *asopao* could make me go home of my own free will. Mami would cook *asopao* again but I would never have appendicitis again, not ever. I didn't have an appendix anymore. This was the last day I could lie here in the morning. The last day I would translate for the doctor who came around at noon and didn't understand what the patient with kidney stones in the next ward was saying. I understood her. I spoke both her language and his. It was my last day to nap with ten other children. The very last day I would get up and play with the dollhouse that I had decorated with mirror ponds and cotton-ball snow.

I said something to Papi in a low voice, I can't remember what. But when

I Didn't Go Home (Christmas 1941)   157

he leaned down to hear better, I remembered the treat in store that Sunday and whispered that the lady from the agency was bringing Christmas gifts to all the children in the wards today, this very afternoon. I turned my head, ashamed. He'd argued so hard with the nurses, worked so hard to get me home early, rules or no rules. But I didn't get up, I didn't back down, and I didn't go home. So when the head nurse came to see me off I was lying with my head turned to the wall, tears sliding down my cheek, my father standing over me, holding my socks and panties in his big, still hands.

Puerto Rican Asopao

In Esmeralda Santiago's family, *asopao* is often the meal after the meal. Her mother, Ramona Santiago, usually makes this soup after everything else has been eaten, the Christmas dishes have been washed, and leftovers have been divided and stored in plastic so that everyone can take a bit of the Christmas meal home. As guests begin to leave the party, Mami offers the *asopao*. This happens every time the family gathers, not just during Navidades, but it's at Christmas when it's most appreciated, as we prepare to battle the cold and snow of life away from Puerto Rico.

4 tablespoons sofrito *(see recipe on page 32)*	1/2 cup white wine
1 tablespoon vinegar	1/2 cup tomato sauce
adobo *(see recipe on following page)*	1/2 cup rice
a 3- to 4-pound chicken, washed, rinsed in lemon juice, dried, and cut up	7 cups water
	1 tablespoon capers
	1 tablespoon Spanish olives, chopped
3 tablespoons olive oil achiote *(see recipe on page 48)*	2 bay leaves
	1/2 teaspoon oregano
	1/2 teaspoon salt

Add 1 tablespoon of the *sofrito* with the vinegar to the *adobo* mixture in a bowl and blend well. Rub the mixture over the chicken pieces. Let marinate in the refrigerator for at least 30 minutes, preferably overnight.

In a soup pot, heat the olive oil *achiote*. Add remaining 3 tablespoons *sofrito*. Cook for 2 minutes.

Add chicken. Cook over medium heat, stirring frequently to ensure that all the pieces of chicken are seasoned. Continue cooking a few minutes more until the chicken is opaque.

Add the white wine and tomato sauce and stir well, then add the rice, water, capers, olives, bay leaves, oregano, and salt. Return the mixture to a boil, then lower heat and simmer, covered, 20 to 25 minutes. Add salt and pepper to taste.

Makes 6 to 8 servings

ADOBO

4 cloves garlic
1 teaspoon peppercorns
1 teaspoon salt

1 teaspoon dried oregano
½ teaspoon paprika

Grind all the ingredients together in a mortar and pestle to make a paste.

Martín Espada

Martín Espada was born in Brooklyn, New York. A recipient of fellowships from the National Endowment for the Arts and the Massachusetts Cultural Council, he is currently Associate Professor of English at the University of Massachusetts, Amherst. His collections of poetry include Imagine the Angels of Bread *(W. W. Norton), which won the American Book Award; and* Rebellion Is the Circle of a Lover's Hands *(Curbstone Press), which was awarded both the Paterson Poetry Prize and the PEN/Revson Fellowship. He is the editor of* Poetry Like Bread: Poets of the Political Imagination from Curbstone Press *and* El Coro: A Chorus of Latino and Latina Poetry. *His poetry has appeared in the* New York Times Book Review, Harper's, The Nation, *and* Ploughshares.

ARGUE NOT CONCERNING GOD

I WAS RAISED by a Puerto Rican father and a Jewish–Jehovah's Witness mother. They met while working at the same factory in Brooklyn; my father was a shipping clerk, my mother a receptionist. Frank Espada was a skeptical and wayward Catholic. Marilyn Levine ate cheeseburgers and expected to be bug-zapped by God for mixing meat and milk in violation of dietary laws.

There is a context for her repudiation of the Jewish faith and identity in favor of a relentlessly proselytizing door-to-door Christian sect most people

find more irritating than a case of ringworm. Sometime between her marriage to my father, in 1952, and my arrival, in 1957, my mother's family disowned her. At age two I glimpsed my mother's father, who escaped from a nursing home. In forty years, this is the only time I can remember meeting anyone on her side of the family, so complete was our ostracism.

Boxed into the Linden projects of East New York with three children in the early 1960s, my mother heeded a stranger at the door selling magazines and prophecy. During my father's regular absences, my siblings and I became, in effect, Witnesses as well. We learned that the Witnesses predicted "the end of this system of things," or Armageddon, a reference to the apocalypse, characterized in the magazines by pictures of crowds shrieking and cowering under a hail of fire. However, the Witnesses always chirped about "the good news" whenever they forecast the tongue-rotting demise of the damned (i.e., anyone not a Jehovah's Witness). After Armageddon came Paradise, like dessert.

Illustrations of Paradise featured somnambulant beneficiaries of eternal life petting equally stupefied lions: Jehovah as taxidermist. The gardens were sterile, the faces numb with narcotic smiles. The Witnesses equated perfection with the deliberately bland, even when they sang. At an early age, I was convinced that their hymns were based on theme songs from television shows. Their aversion to any exuberant or celebratory worship, their awkward austerity, also explained why the Witnesses did not observe Christmas. Of course, millions of people in the United States have no need for this particular holiday; but Christmas, or the lack thereof, became a metaphor for my family's contradictions and illusions.

We celebrated Christmas when I was very young. I can recall swatting my brother into the Christmas tree, which collapsed with the explosion of ornamental bulbs, a detonation of holiday grenades. My parents discovered me untangling my brother, and a great bellowing ensued. (I have learned since that other families also use their Christmas trees as projectiles. My father-in-law once heaved his Christmas tree like a harpoon through a picture window.)

Some time thereafter, my mother announced that she would no longer observe Christmas. She took the official Witness position that Jesus was not actually born on December 25. This was an ancient Roman holiday—a pagan holiday. My father ruled in turn that, if my mother wouldn't celebrate Christmas, then nobody would. This was a family holiday, and if my mother wouldn't celebrate Christmas, then we wouldn't celebrate Christmas *together*, like a family.

However, my father kept his lifelong collection of Christmas ornaments, presumably hoping that my mother would change her mind. My mother made her state of mind very clear one December, a few days before Christmas, during my adolescence. She gathered my father's Christmas ornaments, dropped them in a garbage can, dragged the can to the corner, waited for the trash man to jingle the garbage into his truck, then returned to the house and declared to my father that she had thrown out his treasures.

She did it on his birthday. The Witnesses do not celebrate birthdays, either. This is considered self-exaltation, idol worship. For one day, you are the Golden Calf. Besides, the only two people to have birthday celebrations in the Bible are Pharaoh and Herod. Following this logic, a few balloons and conical party hats may lead the birthday boy or girl to conquer vast deserts and dragoon thousands of slaves to build pyramids.

Thus my mother tossed *Feliz Navidad* into a trash compactor. The argument that followed combined the best features of a theological debate and a cockfight: God, Darwin, screeching, and feathers. I cannot recall my father's words. First his jaw trembled, which was always the prelude to a seismic event. Then the eruption began, his mouth open so wide I swore that I could see his uvula, that tiny punching bag, as if he were a cartoon opera singer.

One of my mother's most frequent quotations from the Bible comes to mind: Jesus said, "I came to put, not peace, but a sword" (Matthew 10:34). Jehovah's Witnesses would cite this verse to justify the breakup of families. Of course, this is the Witnesses' own "New World" translation of the Holy Scriptures. Considering the intricacies of translations from an ancient language, Jesus might well have said, "I came to poach a naughty piece of swordfish."

After my mother's Garbage Offensive, there was no talk of Christmas. My father bought me a duffel bag one year. He told me: "Hey, I'm buying you a duffel bag." To which I replied: "I don't want a duffel bag." He responded: "You're getting a duffel bag." And he gave me a duffel bag, unwrapped, so I would know that it was a duffel bag. Oddly enough, I was not planning on going anywhere.

In high school, I became a Christmas anarchist. I explained the fact that my family didn't celebrate Christmas in revolutionary terms. Christmas was a manifestation of corrupt consumer culture, a capitalist conspiracy, a hypocritical ceremony of the warmongering state. Some of which is no doubt true, though what mattered was the marriage of convenient logic and high sanctimony. I was feeling very spiritual.

But I did not need the Witnesses anymore. My father's arguments for agnosticism and evolutionary theory were ultimately persuasive. My mother's only response to the theory of evolution was, "You may be descended from an ape, but I'm not." My mother's credibility also suffered when the Witnesses predicted "the end" for October 1975, and nothing ended but the baseball season. Moreover, in high school I had discovered girls. One cherubic creature from the local congregation left me with the demeanor of a cow brained by a sledgehammer. I became enamored of this particular headache, and since the Witnesses dictated a code of sexual behavior only a Ken doll could obey, my choices were crystallized.

This is an account of redemption, however. My Christmas history was redeemed by pork: *pernil* in steaming chunks, with slivers of garlic, and *cuero*, the skin that cracked in my squeaking teeth. Every Christmas season during our Brooklyn years, we would travel to the Bronx for dinner at my grandmother's apartment. I was buttoned into my blue suit, a diminutive pallbearer. I then drifted in a Dramamine twilight as the car lumbered through traffic. The only mention of God was my father's litany of "Goddammit! Goddammit!" as we inched down the oxymoronic freeway. Once we arrived in the Bronx, my father would load me with presents for my cousins, and I reeled up five flights of tenement stairs. The door opened on what must have been thousands of Puerto Ricans, all related to me, and the slow dizzy bolero on the record player that left me swaying like a buoy at high tide.

Then came my grandmother's *pernil* with *arroz con gandules*. A boy of generous girth is apt to believe that divinity is a plate of roast pork with rice and pigeon peas. This was the celestial feast. Mysteriously, my grandmother never ate. No one ever saw Tata chew or swallow anything. That was further evidence of the miraculous, a virtual weeping statue in the town plaza.

After dinner my father would organize the family photograph, a gallery of faces with the broad Roig nose, my grandmother's nose and mine, a hill with two caves. My mother posed with the pagan Puerto Ricans, forgetting for the moment that Christmas was not the birthday of Jesus, ignoring the omni-present plaster saints of the Bronx, simply because the pagans insisted on waving her into their snapshots.

My mother is still a Jehovah's Witness. Unlike me, my young son has never heard a debate over whether *his* father is descended from an ape. My wife, born on a Connecticut dairy farm, crafts ornaments by hand and saws down her own Christmas tree in the woods. We celebrate Hanukkah and the Día de Reyes too. Expensive, true, but this year I am planning to moonlight as a professional wrestler to bring in some holiday cash—ring name El Pernil.

I leave the final word to that great Puerto Rican poet, Walt Whitman, from the 1855 introduction to *Leaves of Grass:* "This is what you shall do: Love the earth and sun and the animals, despise riches, give alms to every one that asks, stand up for the stupid and crazy, devote your income and labor to others, hate tyrants, argue not concerning God . . ."

Pernil

ROASTED PORK

The *pernil* is the *lechón* you can't make. Rather than cooking a whole pig (the *lechón*), we cook only the meatiest part, the shoulder roast (*pernil*), which can be easily divided into nice-size portions.

7¹/₂ to 8¹/₂ pounds pork shoulder
    roast
1 teaspoon peppercorns
8 large cloves garlic, peeled
3 teaspoons dry oregano

2 tablespoons salt or to taste
2 tablespoons olive oil
2 tablespoons vinegar
¹/₄ cup sofrito (see recipe on
    page 32)

Wash and dry pork roast. Score meat all around with a sharp knife. Set aside.

Grind peppercorns, garlic, oregano, and salt in mortar and pestle until they form a paste. Add olive oil, vinegar, and *sofrito*, and mash until paste is smooth.

Rub *adobo* over the pork roast, making sure paste goes deep into slits. Place in shallow baking pan, cover tightly, and allow to marinate overnight.

Remove the pork from the refrigerator 30 minutes before cooking. Drain any liquid that may have formed overnight and pour over the pork.

Preheat oven to 300 degrees. Cook for 1 hour. Raise oven temperature to 350 degrees. Cook for another 2 hours or until internal temperature reaches 185 degrees.

Makes 6 to 8 servings

Ilan Stavans

Ilan Stavans grew up in Mexico City. A nominee for the National Book Critics Circle Award and the recipient of a Guggenheim Fellowship and the Latino Literature Prize, he teaches at Amherst College. His many books include The Hispanic Condition *(HarperPerennial),* Art and Anger *and* The Riddle of Cantinflas *(both University of New Mexico Press),* Bandido: Oscar "Zeta" Acosta and the Chicano Experience *(HarperCollins), and* The Oxford Book of Latin American Essays.

OY! WHAT A HOLIDAY!

HANUKKAH IN DISTRITO FEDERAL was a season of joy. The weeklong festival of light was celebrated at home and in school and, indirectly, in our Gentile neighborhood where it was part of the season of *posadas*. Hanukkah almost always fell near Christmas, so many of my holiday memories blend Judas Maccabee with colorful piñatas filled with oranges, *colación*, and bite-sized pieces of sugar cane. In our Yiddish school, we performed humorous *schpiels*, re-enacting the plight of the Hasmoneans who waged a guerrilla war in Palestine in 165 B.C. when the Syrian ruler Antiochus IV desecrated Jerusalem's Holy Temple.

In my young mind, the Jewish resistance became confused with the sorts of uprisings orchestrated by South American left-wing *comandantes*. I pictured the Hasmoneans as Uzi-wielding freedom-fighters in army fatigues.

In one Yiddish-school Hanukkah *schpiel*, I played Judas's father, Mattathias of Modin, sporting a mock beard in the style of Fidel Castro. Another year, in the role of Antiochus, I wore a costume more Spanish conquistador than Old Testament warrior and tried to simulate the voice of Presidente Luis Echeverría Alvarez as I pretended to conquer the Hebrew temple, which in our *schpiel* resembled the pyramid of the sun at Teotihuacán.

During Hanukkah, my parents would give my siblings and me a present each evening. I remember how thrilled I was to receive a beautiful *títere*, a puppet of a humble campesino with a huge mustache, a bottle in one hand, and a pistol in the other. After we opened our gifts, my mother would light another candle in the menorah, placing the candelabra in the dining room window sill.

Our extended family sometimes gathered at my grandmother's house in Colonia Hipódromo for a Hanukkah feast. The cousins sat in circles playing dreidl, spinning the little top, and gambling on how it would fall. No matter how much I prayed for a miracle like the one that swept the Maccabees to redemption, I never managed to win, so that at the end of the evening I was left with no remaining assets to speak of and a bad temper.

After the game, my grandmother served her traditional Jewish-Mexican holiday menu: *pescado a la veracruzana*, chicken soup with *kneidlach*, oven-fried potato latkes topped with *mole poblano* and applesauce. Dessert attempted to evoke the baking style of Eastern European Jewry but were really closer to *típico* Mexican *bizcochos*.

Bellies already overloaded, we ended the evening by joining our neighbors in their *posadas*. Numerous—often awkward—theological questions about the meaning of Judaism would arise.

"Why eight candles?" someone would ask.

"Well, it is because of a *milagro*, a miracle that—"

"Gosh, you guys believe in miracles? The only miracle that ever happened was the one that gave life to our Lord Jesus."

Silence.

"Did you guys really kill Jesus Christ?"

Suddenly, my mind goes blank. "You mean us, personally?"

"Do you Jews consider Him the Messiah?"

"Do you know what the Immaculate Conception is?"

Searching for replies left me with a bizarre, uncomfortable aftertaste. Our Gentile friends never took our answers at face value. Their faces betrayed their puzzlement. No, we had not killed Jesus, nor did we consider him a Messiah but a prophet of biblical dimensions and a nationalistic one at that. Our neighbors accepted us; perhaps a few even loved us—but clearly, they regarded us as creatures from another planet.

I only began to think of my Hanukkah celebrations as "exotic" when I emigrated to Manhattan and described these fiestas to my new American-Jewish friends, whose knowledge of the Hispanic world was limited to a couple of Gabriel García Márquez novels and a weekend in Acapulco. While I was still a child, the thing that struck me most about our Jewish holidays was that they belonged not only to me, a Mexican Jew, but to an endless chain of generations. My parents and teachers had made me an integral part of a small, but transnational and multilingual culture—abstract, marginal, dispersed in corners all over the globe. Millions of kids before me had spun the Hanukkah dreidl and millions more would do so in the centuries to come. I understood that I was just a bridge across an infinite stream. Like all Jewish children, I was a time-traveling Maccabee, re-enacting a cosmic festival of self-definition.

Pescado a la Veracruzana

FILLET OF FISH IN A TOMATO AND ONION SAUCE

This recipe is a family heirloom, graciously sent to us from Mexico City by Ilan Stavan's family, in memory of his grandmother, Miriam Slominski (1912–1991), who prepared it. The dish, a classic of Mexican cuisine, gets its name from the Gulf Coast port city of Veracruz. The term *chile güero* is used for a variety of yellow peppers. Some are hotter than others. The pickled version, found in jars, is usually very mild. Two small fresh chiles give the sauce just a gentle kick. Taste it as it simmers and add more if you like a spicier dish. Simmer the sauce a bit longer if you have the time. After 30 or 40 minutes on the stove, the flavors merge delectably.

2 eggs
2 pounds sea bass fillets (or other
*   firm-fleshed white fish)*
2 cups flour
½ cup corn oil for frying fish
6 onions
7 garlic cloves
parsley (about half a bunch)

5 large tomatoes
1 dry bay leaf
1 bottle pitted green olives
*   (10 ounces), drained*
2 chiles güeros, finely sliced,
*   seeds and veins removed*
salt and pepper to taste

The fish

Lightly beat the eggs in a bowl with a fork. Dredge the fish fillets in the eggs, and then in the flour. Heat the oil in a sauté pan. Finely slice 2 of the onions and 4 of the garlic cloves, and sauté until they just begin to brown. Add the fish, and fry until it turns golden. Drain on paper towels until most of the oil has been absorbed.

The sauce

Slice the remaining onions and garlic cloves, the parsley, and the tomatoes. Chop in a blender or food processor briefly so that the mixture becomes a thick juice. Strain. Heat the strained juice in a saucepan, stirring. Bring to a boil, then reduce heat, add bay leaf, and simmer for 10 minutes. If the mixture becomes too thick, add a little water. Add the olives and sliced chiles. Cook 5 minutes more.

Add the fish to the sauce. Add salt and pepper to taste.

Allow the dish to sit for 5 minutes before serving.

Makes 6 servings

Bizcochitos

❧ MEXICAN ANISE COOKIES

These traditional Mexican pastries are almost identical to an Eastern European Jewish cookie. The Jewish version substitutes poppy seeds for the anise. If you don't like the crunch of seeds in your cookies, you can flavor the sugar by mixing it with the anise. Let it stand overnight, then strain out the seeds before proceeding with the recipe.

2 cups all-purpose flour

1 teaspoon baking powder

2 teaspoons anise seed

½ teaspoon salt

2 sticks (1 cup) unsalted butter, softened

¾ cup granulated sugar

1 large egg

2 tablespoons brandy

cinnamon-sugar (2 parts ground cinnamon to 1 part sugar)

Preheat oven to 350 degrees. Mix the flour, baking powder, anise seed, and salt together in a bowl. Cream the butter and sugar together, add the egg, then the brandy, beating well. Gradually add the dry ingredients and mix well.

Form the dough into a large ball, wrap in plastic wrap, and refrigerate until cold—about 2 hours. (Dough can be made ahead and kept refrigerated.)

Roll the dough out to about ¼ inch thick, and cut into shapes with a knife or cookie cutter. Bake until cookies begin to turn slightly golden—about 20 minutes. Allow to cool just until they can be removed easily from the cookie sheets, then remove onto a platter and sprinkle with cinnamon sugar.

Makes about 2 dozen cookies

Mayra Santos Febres

Mayra Santos Febres was born in Puerto Rico and has won numerous prizes for her fiction, including the 1994 Letras de Oro Prize granted by the University of Miami. She is also the recipient of the Juan Rulfo Prize for short fiction written in Spanish. Her collection of stories, Urban Oracles, *was published in 1997 by Lumen Editions, a division of Brookline Books.*

A LITTLE BIT OF BLISS

IN PUERTO RICO, the Christmas holidays are a long and intense season of greetings and celebrations. They start the night of Thanksgiving and end January 18, after the San Sebastian festival in Old San Juan. Since Puerto Rico has always been a colony, first of Spain and then of the United States, we take the hand-me-down traditions we inherited from both "mother countries" and turn them inside out, transform them into customs that barely resemble what they originally were. In our version of Thanksgiving (a celebration we call Turkey Day) there is no cranberry sauce, no pumpkin pie, no baked yams. Nobody watches the football game, even though we can get it, Eastern time, on cable TV. We keep the turkey, but prepare it with spices that make it taste like traditional holiday pork (we call our invention the *pavochón*). As stuffing, we use ground plantain with lots of garlic and pepper (*mofongo* style). We serve the bird with rice and pigeon peas, *tembleque, morcillas, gandinga,* and other typical foods; colorful, tasty dishes made with leftovers from this and little scraps of that. Our slave food,

our poor campesino food, transforms, through imagination and loving care, into a magical paradise of taste and delight. We do with the food what we do with our traditions, salvage a little morsel of this, add leftovers from that, and piece together a sense of being who we are: Puerto Ricans, painfully happy to be alive.

Christmas Eve is another story. In a way, it is a continuation of the holiday celebrations that start on Turkey Day, but it retains a glow of its own, a special kind of magic. It is another chance to celebrate the time we have spent on the face of this earth with friends and family, those who have had the luck to survive another long year of tribulations. It is an epic celebration, a prize for having won the small battles of everyday life. To reach Nochebuena with your body and soul still able to laugh is no small achievement in any part of the world. Puerto Rico is no exception to the rule.

As children, my brother Juan Carlos and I were filled with apprehension as Christmas Eve neared. That's because our mother, Mariana Febres Falú, was a genuine Christmas-party animal. I don't know why she loved the season so much. Perhaps because she worked so hard the rest of the year, correcting exams, cleaning the house, taking care of my father, my brother and me, and the fact remains that she outdid herself each Christmas.

For days, Mom nagged my father to repaint the house, even if there wasn't a speck of dirt to be discovered on any wall. She dragged us week after week through shopping malls, to find the perfect Christmas decorations. Each year, she organized a party that would be the mother of all parties, and each year she tried to surpass the last. Our neighborhood turned into a mayhem of arches and Christmas lights, and lists were made. Doña Victoria would bring the rum and Doña Olga the *pasteles*, Don Agapito would buy the *lechón* and Don Cheo would arrange the sound system. My aunts would also participate, and my grandmother and cousins. When Christmas Eve arrived we were ready. We had our best dresses on, our best faces on, and our best intentions to celebrate the birth of Christ with a bang, and have the time of our lives.

Now that I think about it, my mother's enthusiasm for Christmas was a bit excessive. Maybe it had to do with her childhood, all those Christmases spent with no food on the table, no lights on the porch, and nothing to celebrate. But she was a Febres woman, and somehow the Febres women found the strength to defeat all obstacles. They seemed invincible. Cruzjosefa,

Cusita, Nena, Cuca, Cuchira, and Mariana. Their dark reddish skin glowed in the sunlight, from the tip of their toes to the base of their necks. Their bodies were towers of clean, sweet-smelling flesh, rising towards the sky. And they knew how to welcome happiness when it arrived, especially at Christmas.

My father was different. He was the only one who could escape my mother's Christmas charm. He did come with us to picnics and school activities, or take us for Sunday drives through the mountains. But he never went to any family gatherings that involved my mother's sisters, especially during Nochebuena. He never explained why. But then again, there were many things my father never explained to us.

Juan Santos was a quiet man. Now he is a preacher. He runs a small Pentecostal church across the street from where he lives with my youngest half-brother, Carlos. But when he was young, he was a fairly successful AA baseball player and a high-school world history teacher. My house was always full of maps, of books explaining Carlo Magno's conquests or the succession of Egyptian pharaohs. He spent hours preparing classes for his students, his hands smelling of ink and burned rubber bands, the dining room table filled with maps and encyclopedias. We used to play a game, the only one he played with us. Some afternoons he sat in the living room, called us at the top of his voice, and drilled Juan Carlos and me about the capitals of the world: "Nicaragua's capital?" he would ask. "Managua!" we would scream out. "Japan's capital?" "Tokyo!" "Czechoslovakia's?" "Prague!" We dreamed of going to those countries with our father, who would ask the names of capitals and tell us stories about civil wars, agricultural production, and archaeological treasures. In those dreams, our father laughed and played many games with us: hide-and-seek in the Parthenon, races up the steps of the Vatican. He would be happy.

From my father's lips I heard for the very first time that Puerto Rico was a colony. We did not have a real capital like Nicaragua, had not fought any war that won us independence. Maybe that was the reason he was so serious all the time, so angry he could not have more, a country to call his own, a place big enough for his standards and dreams of becoming a big man. He argued about politics with my mother, who was pro-Commonwealth, called her a coward colonialist. My mother mocked him. "Ay, *negro*, I am more Puerto Rican than you are. My heart is here, but the money is in the U.S. So what do you want me to do? To starve in the name of freedom? I've starved all my life, and let me tell you it ain't uplifting. There is no freedom in poverty." Then, she would turn the radio on, hike up her short denim pants and go on with the housework. Everything tidy, everything clean. After one of those political arguments, the entire house glowed, the driveway would be spotless, and our uniforms would hang in the closet freshly pressed and waiting to be worn and wrinkled. My mother would sing and mop and dance and water the plants and forget all about my father calling her a coward. Calling her a coward! Now, that was daring! And stupid! If it wasn't for her *cowardice*, we would not be as well-off as we were.

And we were well-off, better than most people who lived on our street. The biggest house in the neighborhood belonged to us, to Mariana and Juan and their two children. The dark-skinned, elegant, intelligent couple of schoolteachers lived at the corner of the street in a big, white house with two cars in which they took their two children to a Catholic private school. They both worked for the pro-Commonwealth government in schools for specially gifted children, a job awarded to those with high connections in the Department of Education. "They have sisters and sisters-in-law working in the mayor's office," the neighbors whispered when we passed by. It was true that my mother's sisters had those high positions in the government and that my aunts pulled strings to help my mother and father get their jobs. But it was also true that my father's hands smelled of burned rubber and chalk, and that my mother's voice was hoarse from screaming multiplication tables all day long. I used to get so angry when I heard the neighbors gossiping about us, but my mother calmed me down. "It's plain envy, baby," she'd say. "Ignore them and smile. Let them know they cannot harm you with their silly comments, that they'll have to try harder to see you cry."

One Christmas Eve, when I was about ten or eleven, my mother and father had a particularly heated argument. We were celebrating Christmas at my grandmother's house that year. All my aunts were coming. The plan was to eat dinner at Grandma's and then go next door to a party we had organized with the next-door neighbors. We would provide the food, and Doña Gladys and Don Agapito the music. Don Agapito had lived most of his life in the city, but he was originally from Cidra, a small town in the mountains. He knew lots of musicians of typical music, those who perform at *lechoneras* and little bars in the mountains, entertaining friends and customers while they ate baked sweet potatoes, *lechón asado,* and drink a couple thousand beers. Don Agapito invited those musicians, especially Don Benny, a taxi driver by day, musician by night. Don Benny had amplifiers, microphones, and all the gadgets for sound equipment, plus a brand-new electronic keyboard and music box that was the sensation of all Cidra. With Don Benny at the party, we were sure to have a blast.

That night, my mother invited my father to come to Don Agapito's party. We were all crammed into the bathroom, my mother and me in front of the big wooden mirror that faced the handbasin. My father stood in the corridor, watching us go about our business. Juan Carlos was half dressed, sitting on the toilet, waiting for my mother to help him find a lost shoe. She was wearing a black halter dress, stockings, and shoes, her hair still in rollers. We were all in a good mood. I was happy because I had managed to convince my parents to let me use lip gloss that night, a banana-flavored one I bought with my own allowance at the corner drugstore. The lip gloss lay on top of the bathroom cabinet, right in front of the big mirror where Mom was brushing my hair. I was very proud of my powers of persuasion that day. To think that I was only eleven, and already capable of convincing my folks to let me wear makeup!

My mother had the Vitapoint ointment in one hand and the big plastic comb in the other. She untangled my hair carefully and then parted it into small sections to braid. I was handing her bobby pins, one by one, and holding two bright white bows in my other hand. Mom would tie them to the end of my braids after she was done. As she finished my second braid, my mother turned to my father.

"*Coño*, Juan, come with us this time," she said. "I didn't get this beautiful to be all alone tonight."

"Are your sisters going to be there?" my father asked, changing the tone of his voice.

"Of course, *negro*," she smiled, absentmindedly.

"Then, I won't go." My father's reply fell into the bathroom like a bucket of cold water. All of a sudden, my mother's eyes changed. I could see them in the mirror. Slowly they filled with a cold fire, a glare that pierced like a large wet knife. They reminded me of Grandma's butcher knife, the one she used to cut chicken's necks whenever she wanted to make fresh *asopao*. I looked at my brother nervously. He just sat on the toilet, minding his own business, unaware of the storm approaching. I guess he thought that this was another of our parents' small fights, a little misunderstanding that would leave an uncomfortable silence roaming about the house for a few hours. A silence my mother would break with her broom and her laughter. But my mother's eyes said something else. Her eyes wanted to cut my father's neck; they would cut him and pull his skin off and throw him into a pot to cook.

My father changed tactics. He mellowed his voice yet maintained a firm position: "Mariana please, don't insist. You know I can't stand your sisters. I'm reminded of them all the time at work. Do I also have to deal with them during Christmas Eve?"

"And that is how you thank them, after all they have done for us?"

"We have earned what we have. We owe nothing to them."

"Come on Juan, you know that's not entirely true."

"Look, Mariana, I'd rather die than spend a night listening to their shouts and tending their parties." He raised his voice, visibly angry. "Who would imagine! Those sisters of yours, so well dressed, such professionals. But put on a record and open a bottle of rum in front of them. What a show! They can't wait to make fools of themselves—"

"Why do you have to talk about my sisters like that?" my mother's voice was sad, but her eyes were getting fiercer and fiercer by the minute. It was hard to believe Dad did not notice her eyes. All he had to do was look in the mirror.

"Papi, stop talking," I muttered. "Stop talking before Mom cuts you with her eyes . . ." But he wouldn't listen. I muttered and muttered, "Stop it, Dad, stop it," very softly, wishing I could use my persuasion skills right then, wishing to have telepathic powers, wishing my banana-flavored lip gloss could turn into a secret microphone through which I could warn my father about my mother's eyes. But he kept on.

"I'm telling the truth. Those sisters of yours are insufferable. And you defend them as if—"

"They're my sisters!" my mother screamed. Mom pulled off her hair rollers, threw them all over the place. She sprinted to the bedroom, found my brother's lost shoe and pushed it onto his foot while she continued screaming, "I'm tired of this shit. All I wanted was to have a good time with my entire family. Is that too much to ask?" She finished dressing Juan Carlos so fast that before I knew it he was standing in the middle of the corridor all combed, dressed and perfumed. "If you don't want to go, there are other ways of saying it. Why do you have to try and fuck up my Christmas?"

"Don't talk dirty in front of the kids," my father yelled.

"I talk dirty all I want!" she screamed and stormed out the door, my brother and I trailing behind. My father just stood there, his arms limp and a blank expression on his face.

My mother's eyes were watery when she opened her Volkswagen. The Volky was blue and shiny and smelled of pine trees, just like Christmas. But we were gloomy and nervous as she pushed us in and drove to Grandma's house. Juan Carlos constantly looked at me, his older sister, as if I had a clue about what we should do next. He expected me to tell him if we should try and console Mom or speak on behalf of our father or jump out of the car to create a crisis that could bring them together again. But what did I know? Why should I be caught in the middle of the drama? All for a stupid party on stupid Christmas Eve at stupid Don Agapito's house.

We arrived at Grandma's. All the sisters were there, the traditional food cooked and served. The musicians began to arrive with their cables, switches, and instrument cases. Everything was happiness and joy, but we were a wreck. My heart was pounding. My brother looked like he would burst into tears at any moment. My mother tried to greet her sisters and neighbors, but her smile came out crooked, stale. I don't remember if our Christmas Eve dinner was good that year, most probably because I didn't eat a bite.

We finished dinner in silence, and sat on Grandma's veranda to watch the musicians prepare their instruments in Don Agapito's terrace. We could see the musicians connecting extensions and testing microphones through the ornamental blocks that separated the terrace from our veranda. Don Benny's huge belly showed between the buttons of his striped shirt, and when he bent over to find the right cables for the amplifier we could see his butt. "Look at Don Benny's piggy bank," my cousins Mayrita and Astrid giggled, pointing at the pale pasty flesh overflowing his pants. At a distance, the hors d'oeuvres trays showed neat patterns of food on a table by the bar. My aunts Cuca and Cusita had carefully arranged the table before we arrived. "To entertain ourselves," Titi Cusita explained. "After we finished Mami's hair, Cuca and I had all this time on our hands."

That night, the air felt fresh and humid, the streets were a little damp from afternoon showers, and the air smelled of ocean spray and orange blossoms from the tree in Grandma's veranda. Soon, the music started playing next door. We got up and helped Grandma look for her glasses and her false teeth and her keys. Once we arrived at Don Agapito's, my mother sat in a corner, drinking a glass of beer. She was shy, a little depressed. Titi Cuchira and Titi Cruzjosefa tried to cheer her up.

"*Muchacha, olvídate de ese tipo.* Don't let him spoil your night. Here, have some *coquito, mamita.* Just a sip."

My mother took a sip of the *coquito,* and a sip of beer and talked with her sisters. Little by little, she smiled again. My brother and I watched as she slowly regained her strut, her groove, her rhythm, and started laughing and greeting newcomers. Don Benny dedicated a song to her, and she pulled Don Agapito to the dance floor.

I couldn't believe my eyes. There she was, my mother, laughing and dancing again. After her eyes wanted to cut my father's throat! After she screeched so hard my chest wanted to explode! How could she be dancing right in front of my eyes, when an hour ago she was screaming and crying and pushing us out the door? What was that all about? My father most probably was at the house, or roaming around in his car, killing time, and alone like always. My mother was here, doing what she always did at family gatherings. Nothing had changed. All that anger and nervousness and pain for nothing!

I walked out of Don Agapito's terrace onto the street and went to sit in my Grandma's veranda. I was in no mood for Christmas Eve. Why should I be? I opened my purse, took out my banana-flavored lip gloss and looked at it for a moment. No messages sent, none received. So I opened the lip gloss and retouched my lips, feeling sorry for myself.

A while later, I saw my mother walking towards me with a smile. "There you are, I was looking all over for you," she said. "Do you want an *alcapurria*? Doña Gladys is frying a fresh batch now." As soon as I looked at her, my eyes filled with tears. I turned my face away, but she saw my watery eyes. Quietly, she sat very close to me and waited. I couldn't speak. So many words jumped to my mouth. I wanted to tell her she did not have to look at my father that way, even if he was a jerk sometimes. I wanted to scream that she shouldn't be so happy, that she should feel sick and confused and bitter, like I was feeling.

But I couldn't speak. All I could do was feel my eyes swell with tears, hold my banana-flavored lip gloss and sit beside her. After a while, Mom spoke.

"Don't you worry. It was just a fight. People fight all the time," she said.

At last my mouth filled with sound. I sobbed. "But parents should not fight, not on Nochebuena."

"Who told you that lie?"

"Nobody fights more than Papi and you. That can't be right, Mami."

"Maybe you're right. But that should not ruin your entire evening. Tonight is Christmas Eve."

"I don't feel like waiting for Christmas anymore."

"Well, you should. You should always wait for happier times. They won't come if you don't wait for them."

"What if they never come, Mami?"

"Oh, they always come. You just have to draw them to you."

"And how do you do that?"

"By laughing and dancing. At first you don't feel you want to bother, but all of a sudden a lightness takes over your steps. And there you go. You are happy again."

"But that's only for a little while, as long as the music plays. But then the party ends and it's over."

"That's all you need, sometimes, a little happiness to get you going. After that, you'll manage on your own," she said as she looked at the sky.

My mother stayed with me a little longer. We looked at the stars, listened to the music, and sang along, sitting on Grandma's porch, *solitas las dos*. When we returned to Don Agapito's terrace, we danced together. I had a great time that night. I even drank some *coquito* that Grandma poured for me into a thimble. I got a little drunk, I think. At the end of the party, I gave Don Agapito a big smack on the cheek. It smelled of coconut, cinnamon, and rum.

"*Mira*, Mariana, this daughter of yours is a little tipsy," he told my mother, laughing.

"*Adiós*, Agapito, what do you expect. She is a Febres girl. *Sandunguera, desde chiquita*. She was born knowing what partying is all about."

Tres Leches

CREAM CAKE

Our friend Luis Miguel Rodríguez Villa gave us this recipe. It was created by his sister, María Cristina Rodríguez de Littke, who won a contest sponsored by Puerto Rico's *San Juan Star* for the best *tres leches* on the island. When we tested it ourselves, we understood why this was the winning entry. It's a very simple version of a dish that can be very complicated to make, and it's sinfully delicious.

THE CAKE

3 eggs	*1 cup all-purpose flour*
1 cup sugar	*1 1/2 teaspoons baking powder*
1/4 cup milk	*1 tablespoon vanilla extract*

Preheat oven to 350 degrees.

Separate the eggs. Beat the egg whites until fluffy. Add the sugar gradually and mix well. Blend in the egg yolks, one at a time. Alternately blend in the milk, flour, and baking powder. Add the vanilla and blend well. Pour into a greased, square baking pan, and bake 45 minutes or until a knife inserted in the cake comes out clean.

Remove the cake from the oven and pierce it with a fork, making little holes evenly over the surface.

Set aside to cool.

THE CREAM FILLING

1 can (14 ounces) sweetened
    condensed milk

1 can (12 ounces) evaporated milk

$^1\!/_2$ cup heavy cream

1 tablespoon vanilla extract

In a large bowl, mix condensed milk, evaporated milk, and vanilla extract until well blended. Slowly pour the mixture over the top of the cake.

THE FROSTING

1 cup whipping cream

Beat whipping cream until stiff. Spread over cake.

Makes 10 to 12 servings

Ray Suárez

Ray Suárez grew up in Brooklyn, New York. The host of National Public Radio's award-winning call-in news program, Talk of the Nation, *he has been a reporter for NBC affiliate WMAQ-TV in Chicago and CBS Radio in Rome, a correspondent for CNN in Los Angeles, and a producer for ABC Radio Network in New York. His work has appeared in the* Washington Post, *the* New York Times, *the* Chicago Tribune, *the* Baltimore Sun, *and other publications. He is the author of* Running Away from Home *(Free Press), a book on white flight and the American city.*

NUESTRA NAVIDAD EN CHICAGO

A FEW DAYS before Christmas, the frost crawled up the inside of our old windows, making it harder to see the sidewalk below. Before we could wipe a window to get a glimpse of the park, an incongruous sound carried across the frigid, still air.

Two guitars, maracas, a *güiro*, and a small crowd trying to keep up with the songs were heading toward our house. The yellow glow of modern streetlights bounced off a brand-new dusting of snow. Our friends, laughing and threading their way across the whitened park, sent up little breath-cloud plumes against the bright light. Christmas was arriving in the form of these frozen musicians and their chilled chorus, and we could watch it all for another minute before running to open the door.

Usually by this time of year my wife and I would have long since made our reservations for the flight back to New York. Virtually every Christmas we had followed a star back to Brooklyn. From London, Rome, Los Angeles, or Chicago, we always managed, a few days before, on the eve, or unpardonably early on Christmas morning, when Kennedy and La Guardia are quiet as tombs. One relative or another could always be prodded into sleepily heading over the Brooklyn-Queens Expressway to pick us up.

This Christmas we were confined; my wife, as the King James Version would say, was "great with child," our first. We had been renovating, as cash would permit, an eighty-five-year-old faded beauty facing a small park. Palmer Square was home to successive waves of Chicagoans since it was first developed in the early years of the century. The Norwegian, Swedish, and German petit bourgeoisie had given way to Ukrainians, Russian Jews, and Poles, and eventually to Puerto Ricans, Cubans, and a sprinkling of Latinos from clear down to Tierra del Fuego.

In the closing years of the 1980s, Puerto Ricans and, increasingly, Mexicans were buying and fixing small houses on side streets off the broad, beautiful boulevard that ran like a ribbon through the neighborhood. The houses had two or three apartments, making it feasible to split the mortgage with a cousin, brother, or sister.

Beautiful graystones, from the years on either side of the First World War, were available at prices impossible to find in other, more gentrified sections of town. So a new class of Latino yuppies, not scared of the neighborhood's Spanish-speaking ambience, began drifting in from the Lakefront.

There we were, often the first people in our families to head for college, pick up degrees, and march into big corporations. Sure, Latinos had worked down in the Loop for years, but they had been heavily concentrated—some would say confined—in the hotel and restaurant business.

At the same time, we were still who we were. Many born there, others born here. The Ecuadoran MBA and the Mexican-American real estate agent, the Colombian municipal-contracts supervisor and the Mexican-American not-for-profit manager, Puerto Ricans born here who spoke English with an accent, and Puerto Ricans born there who spoke Spanish with an accent. We were clustered in our late thirties, political, ambitious, angry, and affectionate.

We found each other, through the bush telegraph of political fund-raisers and community agency open houses and friendships formed in college. We sought out each other's company, babysat, shared bottles of wine, and sang "Happy Birthday." Now it was Christmas. Somebody said, "How about a *parranda?*" We had all laughed. *Parranda* was a lovely custom, more suited to a low-rise tropical world of villages and small towns. It was a custom that might not be expected to travel any better than the *coquí*, the Puerto Rican frog said to die when it is taken off the island.

Musicians singing traditional *aguinaldos* would wander from house to house, expecting to find hospitality, both solid and liquid, at every stop. The *parrandistas* literally sang for their supper, accompanied by the householders and a growing entourage of friends, neighbors, and relatives, on- or off-key. It is a beautiful custom, quite in tune with that old and perhaps vanishing Puerto Rico, where people not only knew all their neighbors but all their neighbors' business, as well.

In late-twentieth-century Chicago, we had to find a broader definition of kinship. We were amalgam people. Our *parranda* would meld the warmth and welcome we believed was our birthright with the caution of the new proprietors we had struggled so hard to become. Not everyone who decided they'd like to join in would be welcome.

There would be more surrenders. Now thirty-eight weeks pregnant, there was no way Carole was going to cook the labor-intensive dishes of the season: *pasteles*, mashed plantain stuffed with pork; *pollo guisado*, chicken and vegetables in red sauce; *pastelillos*, fried meat pies. No, these would be—sorry, Abuela—bought from Sabor Latino, one of a cluster of struggling, undercapitalized, and occasionally wonderful small restaurants in our neighborhood.

Invitations were spit out of desktop-publishing programs. Homes were decorated. Food was ordered. Booze was acquired. A few days before the party, a cold front came barreling down from Canada, promising to make this one of the coldest Christmases in a generation. Perfect. Just the thing to remind us we weren't on the island anymore.

Phone calls followed. Should we move from house to house? Should the pregnant women (three of them) go by car while the first ever Iditarod *parranda* proceeded by snowshoe? We stuck with our plan. A frozen delivery man from Sabor Latino arrived an hour later than expected, but before the guests (also late) arrived from their first stop around the corner.

Candles were lit. Lights dimmed. The house began to fill with the bouquet of vast amounts of Puerto Rican food. We stood by the frosty windows and waited for the bell. Leaving the door open was out of the question in single-digit cold. Musicians and revelers and, yes, even pregnant women climbed the stairs, their faces flushed scarlet and their eyes shining. The songs continued in the living room.

The Anglos scattered through the room, friends, neighbors, spouses, and lovers sipped their drinks and smiled indulgently, some limbering up their high-school Spanish and consulting the song sheets, drinking the whole thing in. This is what the potent combination of migration and education brings.

It was a cornerstone belief of the Latinos in the room that something beyond merely liking each other bound us together. We looked for the similarities in family histories, the struggles of the newly landed, and our ongoing argument with America about being here. There was the bond of religion (though many were indifferent Catholics, even outright atheists). There was the bond of Spanish (though there was a range in facility from poetic fluency to something hard on the ear). Time in the States ranged from a few years to a few generations to South Texans who had been in the country as long as there had been one.

Yet somehow we were all *raza*. More sentimental than hardheaded? Maybe. Was this notion of identity so plastic we could easily bend it to fit our needs? Perhaps. But here in this city so far from the places where the Giraldos and the Laras and the Martínezes and the Garcías and the Suárezes started their journeys, we didn't need to analyze all this very much. We saw ourselves in each others' eyes, and that was enough. For those of us far from home and the people who shared our names and our DNA, this was as good a family as we could find on the road. For this holiday, we had created a warm country to live in. It was Christmas in Pan-America, and though there would never be a special on TV for our new nation, we had a feeling we were all on our way to a different somewhere than the place where we started out.

Pitorro, a Puerto Rican grappa found more often in well-washed plastic bleach containers than in fancy bottles, emerged from someone's coat. Despite a hurried life, I found time to make pitchers of *coquito*. The songs continued. The Three Kings on the mantel stared across the living room at the silently winking Christmas tree.

When the *parrandistas* made their way to the next house, we took a deep breath. Alone again, we began to clean up. After bouncing around a lot through our married life, we were home. We cared about these people, and were happy to have a house full of them.

Late on El Día de los Tres Reyes, the contractions began. I packed away the Christmas ornaments while Carole labored, knowing that soon there would be very little time for these chores. The deep chill had kept its grip on Chicago through Christmas and into the young New Year. We drove through quiet, cold streets the next morning to the hospital, and Rafael was in our arms just a few hours later. He was too late for the party, and right on time.

Coquito

COCONUT EGGNOG

When he sent us this recipe, Ray Suárez included the following instructions: "If you are a hard-ass, a traditionalist, or an *Independentista*, you must begin by preparing coconut milk from scratch with a whole coconut and a hammer. You've got to soak the meat, strain it in cheesecloth, and set it aside. Otherwise you can buy packaged coconut, soak it, and drain the pulp from the liquid. Or you can do the easiest thing of all—buy canned coconut milk (sorry). You cannot prepare this recipe in advance, because it's just not a good idea with raw eggs (salmonella threat). If you want to get a jump in your frantic last-minute preparations, I suggest you mix up the *coquito* not much more than 2 hours beforehand. Since I always end up drinking this with people I really love, I suggest you do the same."

1 can (14 ounces) coconut milk
2 cups good white rum (you could use mediocre rum, but why?)
4 egg yolks

1 can (12 ounces) condensed milk
1 1/4 tablespoons ground nutmeg or cinnamon (1/4 tablespoon for the drink, 1 tablespoon for garnish)

Mix all the ingredients in a blender, and blend at very high speed for over a minute. Chill in the refrigerator for 1 to 2 hours. Shake well, and serve.

Makes 10 to 15 servings

EL ASALTO

The Holiday Assault

LIKE THE *posadas* of Mexico, the *parrandas* of Puerto Rico go from house to house singing traditional Christmas songs. The best *parrandas* take you by surprise. Known as *el asalto*, the assault, the idea is that the targeted hosts should be fast asleep when the musicians appear at the door asking to be let in and given a drink (specifically, rum). Anytime during the Christmas season (early December to Three Kings Day on January 6), a family that retires early can expect to wake up in the wee hours to the sound of neighbors strumming a *cuatro* or guitar, scratching a *güiro*, shaking maracas, and singing.

There are many verses to the *El Asalto* song, often improvised on the spot by the musicians and/or the hosts. The song reproduced here is one of many variations. The first verse, repeated as a chorus, announces the musicians' surprise visit. "If you don't have rum," they sing, "send for it." The visitors then ask to be let in. "Nochebuena," they remind the hosts, "is a night for feasting." When the door is opened and the *parranda* has moved inside, the musicians promise a night of celebration. "Navidades is for dancing," they state. After everyone has danced and had their fill of food and drink, the *parranda* moves on to another house, often joined by the hosts of the previous *asaltos*.

Este es el asalto, este es el asalto
De la Navidad.
Si no tiene el trago, mándelo a buscar.
Si no tiene el trago, mándelo a buscar.

Levante compadre,
Levante compadre
Y ábranos la puerta
Que la Nochebuena,
Es noche de fiesta,
Que la Nochebuena,
Es noche de fiesta.

Este es el asalto, este es el asalto
De la Navidad.
Si no tiene el trago, mándelo a buscar.
Si no tiene el trago, mándelo a buscar.

Pensamos cantarle,
Pensamos cantarle
Hasta que amanezca.
Levante compadre
Y ábranos la puerta.
Levante compadre
Y ábranos la puerta.

Este es el asalto, este es el asalto
De la Navidad. . . .

Ya estamos adentro,
Ya estamos adentro,
Vamos a gozar.
Que las Navidades
Son para bailar.
Que las Navidades
Son para bailar.

Este es el asalto, este es el asalto
De la Navidad. . . .

Sírvase un palito,
Sírvase un palito
Para calentar.
Pa' que mi garganta
Se pueda aclarar.
Pa'que mi garganta
Se pueda aclarar.

Este es el asalto, este es el asalto
De la Navidad. . . .

Acknowledgments

WE HAD AN EXTENDED Christmas this year, full of surprises and high emotions. The months we spent organizing this book stretched the holiday, kept us humming *aguinaldos* through the humid days of August and beyond, as the leaves changed color and then dropped to form a thick carpet on the ground. Throughout the summer and fall we received wonderful gifts: stories, poems, treasured recipes, and songs—the legacy of traditions kept alive through the willpower of people unwilling to forget their heritage.

We are deeply grateful to the twenty authors, some of whom were immersed in novels or other long works in progress, who stopped to remember. Our humble thanks to the *mamis*, the aunts and in-laws, the relatives often more than once removed, who for the first time in their lives measured ingredients as they cooked so that we could present their recipes in an easy-to-duplicate form.

Mil gracias to Laura, Jennifer, Emily, and Daniel Cohen, Sandra, Essie, and Alex Cohen, Francesca and Miranda Jones, Karen Dressner, Judith Azaña, Ginger Varney, and Ila Cantor, who chopped, crushed, stirred, wrapped, sautéed, fried, and baked as we tested the recipes. Steven and Laura Cohen opened their home to us, gave us free rein in their spacious kitchen, and confirmed that the qualities we associate with Christmas—generosity, celebration of life, family ties, friendship, traditions, and fun—can be daily miracles to be treasured.

Two special friends, our agent, Molly Friedrich, and our editor, Robin Desser, not only nurtured the book along, but also joined the cooks and the revelers during the memorable cook-a-thon that brought Las Navidades to Westchester County a month early. Now they can both wrap *pasteles* and tamales like experts.

Esmeralda's husband, Frank Cantor, in true cinema verité fashion, braved the craziness in the test kitchens to create a memorable video of us looking by turns frazzled, elated, and exhausted, while Lucas Cantor soothed us with his jazz guitar.

Finally, our heartfelt thanks to Eileen Rosaly for introducing us to each other. That meeting resulted not only in a joyful collaboration, but in a wonderful friendship.

ESMERALDA AND JOIE

Permissions Acknowledgments

Grateful acknowledgment is made to the following for permission to reprint previously published material:

Doubleday: "Good Night to *Nochebuena*" excerpted from *Next Year in Cuba: A Cubano's Coming of Age* by Gustavo Pérez Firmat, copyright © 1995 by Gustavo Pérez Firmat. Reprinted by permission of Doubleday, a division of Bantam Doubleday Dell Publishing Group, Inc.

Judy Vásquez: "Jíbarismos" by Judy Vásquez, copyright © 1997 by Judy Vásquez (*El Boricua*, December 1997). Reprinted by permission of the author.

A Note About the Illustrator

JOSÉ ORTEGA was born in Ecuador in 1965 and graduated from the School of Visual Arts in 1988. The recipient of numerous awards for a wide range of work, he currently lives in New York City.